I0004687

# CSS Development (with CSS3!)

# CSS Development (with CSS3!)

Zachary Kingston

LearnToProgram, Inc.
Vernon, Connecticut

LearnToProgram.tv, Incorporated
27 Hartford Turnpike Suite 206
Vernon, CT 06066
contact@learntoprogram.tv
(860) 840-7090

©2013 by LearnToProgram.tv, Incorporated

ISBN-13: 978-0-9888429-9-1
ISBN-10: 0988842998

All rights reserved. No part of this document may be reproduced or transmitted in any form or by any means, electronic, mechanical, photocopying, recording, or otherwise, without prior written permission of LearnToProgram.tv, Incorporated.

*Limit of Liability/Disclaimer of Warranty*: While the publisher and author have used their best efforts in preparing this book, they make no representations or warranties with respect to the accuracy or completeness of the contents of this book and specifically disclaim any implied warranties of merchantability or fitness for a particular purpose. No warranty may be created or extended by sales representatives or written sales materials. The advice and strategies contained herein may not be suitable for your situation. You should consult with a professional where appropriate. By following the instructions contained herein, the reader willingly assumes all risks in connection with such instructions. Neither the publisher nor author shall be liable for any loss of profit or any other commercial damages, including but not limited to special, incidental, consequential, exemplary, or other damages resulting in whole or part, from the readers' use of, or reliance upon, this material.

Mark Lassoff, Publisher
Kevin Hernandez, VP/ Production
Alison Downs, Copy Editor
Alexandria O'Brien, Book Layout
Niaz Makhdum, Technical Writer
Jeremias Jimenez, Technical Editor

Dedication

To my family.

# TABLE OF CONTENTS

Chapter 1 Welcome to CSS ................................................................. 13
1.1 Introducing CSS .......................................................................... 13
1.2 Modifying Hello World ............................................................... 17
1.3 CSS Selectors ............................................................................. 25
1.4 The 3 Ways to Deploy CSS .......................................................... 36
1.5 Introducing CSS3 ....................................................................... 43
*Questions for Review* ....................................................................... *49*
Chapter 2 Styling Specific Elements ................................................. 51
2.1 Styling Text Elements ................................................................. 51
*Code Listing: Poem Page HTML* ....................................................... *52*
*Code Listing: Story Page HTML* ....................................................... *58*
*Questions for Review* ....................................................................... *66*
2.2 Styling Tables and Lists .............................................................. 67
*Code Listing: Styling Tables HTML* .................................................. *67*
*Code Listing: Styling Tables CSS* ..................................................... *73*
*Questions for Review* ....................................................................... *77*
2.3 Styling Backgrounds .................................................................. 78
*Questions for Review* ....................................................................... *86*
2.4 The Sliding-Door Technique (Making a CSS Button) ................. 87
*Questions for Review* ....................................................................... *94*
2.5 Sprite Sheets and Images ............................................................ 95
*Code Listing: Sprite Sheet Setup* ...................................................... *97*
*Code Listing: Sprite Sheet Final HTML* ............................................ *102*
*Code Listing: Sprite Sheet Final CSS* ............................................... *103*
*Questions for Review* ....................................................................... *105*
2.6 Creating a Drop-Down Menu with CSS ..................................... 106
*Code Listing: Drop-Down Menu Setup* ............................................. *107*
*Code Listing: Drop-Down Menu CSS* ............................................... *115*
*Questions for Review* ....................................................................... *116*
Chapter 3 The Box Model ................................................................ 119
3.1 Introduction to the Box Model .................................................. 119
*Code Listing: Intro to the Box Model HTML* ..................................... *121*
*Code Listing: Intro to the Box Model CSS* ........................................ *122*
*Questions for Review* ....................................................................... *128*
3.2 The Content Area ...................................................................... 129
*Code Listing: Content Area Example HTML* ...................................... *129*
*Code Listing: Content Area Example CSS* ......................................... *130*
*Questions for Review* ....................................................................... *139*
3.3 Border and Outline Styling ........................................................ 140
*Questions for Review* ....................................................................... *149*
3.4 Working with Margins and Padding ........................................... 150
*Code Listing: Margins & Padding HTML* ........................................... *151*

   *Code Listing: Margins & Padding CSS*..................................*156*
   *Questions for Review*..................................*157*
**Chapter 4 Animations with CSS3** ..................................**161**
**4.1 CSS3 Transforms** ..................................**161**
   *Code Listing: Transforms HTML*..................................*162*
   *Code Listing: Transforms CSS*..................................*163*
   *Questions for Review*..................................*175*
**4.2 CSS3 Transitions** ..................................**176**
   *Code Listing: Transitions HTML*..................................*177*
   *Code Listing: Transitions CSS*..................................*178*
   *Questions for Review*..................................*184*
**4.3 CSS3 Animations** ..................................**185**
   *Code Listing: Animated Color Box CSS* ..................................*186*
   *Code Listing: Animations HTML*..................................*188*
   *Code Listing: Animated Sprite CSS*..................................*189*
   *Questions for Review*..................................*192*
   *Chapter 4 Lab Solutions*..................................*194*
   *Lab Solution HTML*..................................*194*
   *Lab Solution CSS* ..................................*195*
**Chapter 5 Putting Elements Together** ..................................**199**
**5.1 The Display Property** ..................................**199**
   *Code Listing: Display HTML* ..................................*200*
   *Code Listing: Display CSS* ..................................*201*
   *Questions for Review*..................................*207*
**5.2 In-Depth CSS Positioning** ..................................**208**
   *Questions for Review*..................................*217*
**5.3 Floating Elements** ..................................**218**
   *Code Listing: Float Element HTML*..................................*218*
   *Code Listing: Float Element CSS*..................................*220*
   *Questions for Review*..................................*229*
   *Chapter 5 Lab Solutions*..................................*232*
   *Lab Solution HTML*..................................*232*
   *Lab Solution CSS* ..................................*232*
**Chapter 6 CSS for Mobile** ..................................**237**
**6.1 Testing Webpages on Mobile Devices**..................................**237**
   *Downloading the Mobile Testing Environment*..................................*239*
   *Questions for Review*..................................*245*
**6.2 Elegant CSS for the Mobile World**..................................**246**
   *Code Listing: Pre-Mobile Friendly HTML*..................................*247*
   *Code Listing: Pre-Mobile Friendly CSS*..................................*249*
   *Questions for Review*..................................*262*
   *Lab Solutions HTML*..................................*264*
   *Lab Solutions CSS*..................................*265*
**Answer Key: CSS Development (with CSS3!)**..................................**267**
**Appendix: CSS Rules or Terms** ..................................**273**

About the Author

Zachary Kingston is a software developer working out of Winooski, Vermont. He enjoys Vermont culture, getting outdoors, and code that clearly should not work but does anyway. Zach graduated from Clarkson University in 2012, where he played rugby and studied Computer Science and Psychology. As an educator, Zach hopes to help lower the barrier of entry into the wide world of software systems.

Courses Available from LearnToProgram, Inc.

HTML and CSS for Beginners (with HTML5)
Javascript for Beginners
C# for Beginners
jQuery for Beginners
iOS Development Code Camp
Become a Certified Web Developer
PHP & MySQL for Beginners
iOS Development for Beginners
Objective C for Beginners
C Programming for Beginners
Android Development for Beginners
Creating an MP3 Player with Adobe Flash
AJAX Development
Python for Beginners
CSS Development (with CSS3)
HTML5 Mobile App Development with PhoneGap


Books from LearnToProgram, Inc.

HTML and CSS for Beginners
Create Your Own MP3 Player with HTML5

Note: In order to follow along with some exercises outlined in this book please download images and files from:

http://www.learntoprogram.tv/book/CSSDev.zip

# CHAPTER 1

# WELCOME TO CSS

## CHAPTER OBJECTIVES:

- You will learn the overall functions of CSS and how an external CSS file is used to effectively design and modify an HTML page.
- You will be able to understand the different types of CSS selectors and how to use them.
- You will see how CSS gives preference to specific rules when more than one is used at once.
- You will understand the three different methods used to deploy CSS on your webpage.

## 1.1 INTRODUCING CSS

Cascading Style Sheets, which is abbreviated as **CSS**, is a web development language that allows you to determine the visual appearance of HTML pages in popular web browsers like Internet Explorer, Mozilla Firefox, Google Chrome, and Safari. Using CSS, we can create webpages that are more aesthetically pleasing, more user-friendly, and even more intuitive than we could do otherwise.

CSS is traditionally used to improve the appearance of webpages by attaching style code to the web pages' HTML elements. CSS is also used to design the look of documents when they are viewed in other media, e.g.: you can decide how the webpage will look when it is displayed in a projector, or when it is printed.

Before we jump right into the details of CSS code and structure, let's talk about the role of CSS in modern web development. It should also be mentioned that before moving forward with CSS, you need to be totally comfortable with HTML code.

> **TIP:** If you need to refresh your memory on HTML, you might want to check out **HTML and CSS for Beginners (with HTML5)** by Mark Lassoff, published by LearnToProgram, Inc. Check out www.LearnToProgram.tv and click on 'Books'.

In the standard web development model, the backbone of the webpage is written with HTML. HTML provides the structure of the document. When we need to add interactivity, we can do it with a client side programming language like Javascript or a server side programming language like PHP. With CSS, we can decide how a page will actually appear in the browser. If HTML and the client/server side programming are the engine and the wheels of our webpages, CSS is the body and the paint job.

For example, let's consider the following webpage, Google.com. Google.com is the homepage of internet's most successful search engine. This webpage is elegant, and most importantly, it is intuitive and easily accessible. Users visit Google for one reason only: to search for something on the web. Google is set up with the search bar located conveniently right in the middle of the page so you can never miss it.

Figure 1.1: The Google home page viewed in the Firefox browser in Windows.

If you remove CSS from the Google.com page, you can see a skeleton of the webpage, as shown in the following figure. You will be able to see that the page, on a technical level, will not lose its functionality—the hyperlinks and the text boxes and buttons will appear and be functional. However, the overall structure and beauty of the webpage is lost.

**Figure 1.2:** The Google home page viewed without the benefit of CSS code. Notice the disjointed appearance of the page.

One of the unique challenges of web development is that the end user—the person visiting your website—could be doing so using a variety of browsers. It's increasingly likely that your site visitors will be browsing from a mobile device. Since you definitely want all users to have the same experience, you will want your website to look the same no matter what browser or device is used to access it. To ensure this, the W3C, or the World Wide Web Consortium, sets specific standards for how code is interpreted by browsers. They publish these standards, which are specifications that all major web browsers must adhere to if they would like to remain relevant and accepted by users. A browser that doesn't follow the W3C standards would interpret code differently than a standards-based browser and provide an inconsistent experience for the user.

Now is really a great time for you to learn CSS, because CSS2 (which has been around for over a decade) is actually in the process of being phased out and replaced by a newer version, CSS3. However, this isn't going to happen all at once. W3C uses a module development style where portions of CSS3 are introduced slowly over time. As of right now, CSS3 Color, Namespaces and Selectors are on the official list of recommendations. However, browsers implement these modules generally before they are officially recommended by W3C. What this means for you, as a developer, is that you can use CSS3 styles before they are part of the official standard. Talk about being cutting edge!

**CSS2**

**CSS3**

I hope you will find that CSS is really a fun technology to learn because every new skill that you develop in CSS has an immediate visual reward. This should help you stay motivated and excited while learning CSS.

# 1.2 MODIFYING HELLO WORLD

In this section we're going to start writing actual CSS code. You will use CSS to add color and a bit of formatting to an existing HTML page. To begin working in CSS you will need two things, the first of which is a text editor.

> You can use Notepad++ as an efficient text editor, which is easily downloadable for free at http://notepad-plus-plus.org/.

I enjoy using this editor because it is minimal in its presentation, but does support syntax highlighting for both HTML and CSS. In reality, any text editor will be fine, however, you should stay away from word processors like Microsoft Word or Open Office writer. These programs will add formatting and versioning information to the text you create, which will confuse the web browsers when they attempt to interpret your code. The second item that you will need to test CSS code is a web browser, like Mozilla Firefox or Google Chrome.

**Avoid using word processors that will add formatting, like Microsoft Word or Open Office**

Key the following code into your text editor:

```
<!DOCTYPE html>
<html>

<head>
</head>

<body>
    <h1>The Hello World Page</h1>
    <p>Hello World!</p>

</body>
</html>
```

Now save this code in a file, and name it *helloworld.html*. This is just HTML's basic document structure with a heading and paragraph element added to the body of the document. If all is coded correctly, when loaded in to a web browser, the file should appear like this:

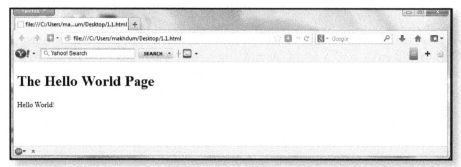

Figure 1.3: The view in the browser where the simple 'hello world' HTML code is implemented.

You can style the document by adding CSS code in the following way:

```
<!DOCTYPE html>
<html>

<head>
<style type="text/css">
    h1{
            color: red;
            text-align: center;
        }

</style>
</head>

<body>
    <h1>The Hello World Page</h1>
    <p>Hello World!</p>

</body>
</html>
```

After adding the CSS code, it will appear in the web browser like this:

Figure 1.4: The browser view where the header element is colored and aligned in the center.

Here you can see that the header element is colored in red, and its position is fixed in the center of the page, as defined in the style element in the document's header.

Let's analyze the CSS portion of the code. The HTML style tag is used here to place the CSS directly in the HTML header section. To tell the browser interpreting this page what kind of styling language you are using, you should start by adding the following, using the type attribute:

```
<style type="text/css">
```

> **NOTE:** The new HTML5 W3C specification does not require that the type attribute is used. We've included it here because most developers still put it in out of habit and it certainly doesn't affect the outcome if you do decide to use the attribute.

It's time to analyze our first CSS rule. The CSS code itself must appear between style tags. Each CSS rule has specific parts. The first part indicates which HTML element the rule is going to affect. We will start by telling the browser that this rule will be applied to the h1 element. In CSS when you write h1 to indicate that you want the CSS styles to apply to all h1 tags, it is called a selector.

```
h1{

    }
```

We're going to use the color style to modify the color of all h1 elements. We've used the value red to indicate which color we desire.

```
color: red;
```

In addition to changing the color, you can change the alignment of the element. In this example we are aligning the content to the center:

```
text-align: center;
```

You can also color the text in the paragraph element using the following code:

```
<html>
<head>

<style type="text/css">

    h1{
        color: red;
        text-align: center;
        }

    p{
        color: rgb(255,0,255);   /*purple*/
        }
</style>
</head>
<body>
    <h1>The Hello World Page</h1>
    <p>Hello World!</p>

</body>
</html>
```

In the browser, you will see the following:

**Figure 1.5:** The browser view where you can observe the purple-colored paragraph element.

Here, a more robust method of coloring the elements is used, which is the function rgb(), which lets us to determine the color using the RGB color system. The following code results in a purple color:

```
color: rgb(255,0,255);   /*purple*/
```

In this style rule there are three parameters. Each can hold a value between 0 and 255. The first value indicates the amount of red, the second, the amount of green and, the third, the amount of blue in the color. For purple, the value is (255,0,255), which means equal amounts of red and blue. You may also represent the color using a more technical option, which are hexadecimal (aka hex) values:

```
color:#ff00ff;
```

The hexadecimal color system is based on 16 single digits, unlike the decimal system that you're used to which is based on 10. If we were to count to 16 using hex values it would look like this:

0, 1, 2, 3, 4, 5, 6, 7, 8, 9, A, B, C, D, E, F.

We can make any number up to 255 by combining hex digits. FF is the hex equivalent of 255.

If you want to color the paragraph element in blue, you would write the following:

```
color: #0000ff;   /*blue*/
```

In the browser, it will look like this:

Figure 1.6: The paragraph element is colored blue.

Using **comments**, we can tell the browser to ignore certain portions of text when parsing the code. This allows us to write small remarks in the code that may later serve as reminders to ourselves or other developers using our code.

Here, we use /* and */ to begin and end the comment. You can write anything in between /* and */ as a comment, and it will be ignored by the browser. Please also note that the CSS system of commenting is different than the commenting system used in HTML.

/* comments */

If you want to modify the background of your page and give it a blue color, then your code should be written like this:

```
<html>
<head>

<style type="text/css">

    body{
         background-color: rgb(0,0,200);
/*blue*/
         }

    h1{
         color: red;
         text-align: center;
```

```
        }

    p{
        color: rgb(255,0,255);   /*purple*/
        }
</style>
</head>
<body>
    <h1>The Hello World Page</h1>
    <p>Hello World!</p>

</body>
</html>
```

When viewed in the browser, the result will look like this:

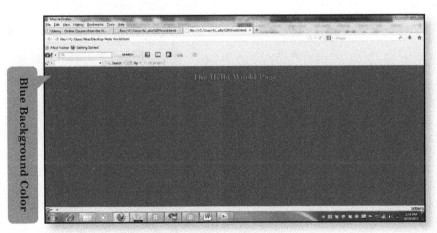

Figure 1.7: Background color is applied in the webpage.

If you were to write the following code:

```
p{
color: rgb(0,0,255);   /*blue*/
color: #ff00ff;    /*purple*/
}
```

You will see that the "hello world!" text in the paragraph portion will appear purple. While this is a simple example, this is the first example of the "Cascade" in CSS. CSS gives preference to the rules that are more specific, or that have been declared after a previous rule. For example, the paragraph element would be blue if we were to reverse the order in the following way:

```
p{
color: #ff00ff;     /*purple*/
color: rgb(0,0,255);  /*blue*/
}
```

# 1.3 CSS SELECTORS

CSS selectors allow us to accurately target elements and ranges of elements with the CSS rules.

Let us consider the following HTML code:

```
<!DOCTYPE html>
<html>

<head>
</head>

<body>
    <h1>The Selectors Page (This Text is
Italic!)</h1>

    <p>Red</p>
    <p>Red and Bold</p>
    <p>Red</p>

    <ul>
        <li><p>Blue and Bold</p></li>
        <li><p>Blue</p></li>
        <li><p>Blue</p></li>
        <li><p>Blue and Bold and Italic</
p></li>
        <li><p>Blue <p>Red</P> </p></li>
        <li><p>Blue</p></li>
        <li><a>Blue</a></li>
    </ul>

    <p>Red Red Red Red Red Red Red Red Red
Red Red Red Red Red Red Red</p>

    <p>This text is Green, usually.</p>
```

```
    </body>

    </html>
```

If viewed in the browser without the benefit of CSS styling, the result will appear like this:

Figure 1.8: Here you can see a header and some paragraph elements, including some list elements.

Now, let us add some of the previously mentioned CSS rules to our code:

```
<!DOCTYPE html>
<html>

<head>
```

*CSS Development (with CSS3!)*

```
<style type="text/css">

    p,a{
        color: red;
        }

    li > p{
        color: blue;
          }

    .bold{
        font-weight: bold;
        }

    .ital{
        font-style: italic;
        }

    #special{
        color: green;
            }

    #special: hover{
        color: purple;
            }
</style>
</head>

<body>
    <h1 class="ital">The Selectors Page
(This Text is Italic!)</h1>

    <p>Red</p>
    <p class="bold">Red and Bold</p>
    <a>Red</a>

    <ul>
```

```
         <li> <p class="bold">Blue and
Bold</p> </li>
         <li> <p>Blue</p> </li>
         <li> <p>Blue</p> </li>
            <li> <p class="bold ital">Blue
and Bold and   Italic</p> </li>
         <li> <p>Blue</p> </li>
         <li> <p>Blue</p> </li>
         <li> <p>Blue</p> </li>
   </ul>

   <p>Red Red Red Red Red Red Red Red Red
Red Red Red Red Red Red Red</p>
   <a>Red Red Red Red Red Red Red Red Red
Red Red Red Red Red Red Red</a>
   <p id="special">This text is Green,
usually.</p>

</body>
</html>
```

Viewed in the browser now, the result will look like this:

**Figure 1.9:** Notice that the header element is italicized and the paragraph elements are colored accordingly .

In addition to header elements, pages are also composed of paragraphs and anchor elements (among others). Generally with CSS rules, you want to work in broad general cases, and then style for specific rules as they come. To make all paragraph and anchor elements red, we could write the following code:

```
p{
  color: red;
  }

a{
  color: red;
  }
```

If we write a separate rule for the paragraph and anchor elements as shown, the code will actually be more complex than is necessary. If you want to modify the rule, you will have to make the changes in both the paragraph selector and the anchor selector. So, to be more efficient, you should write the code in the following way:

```
p,a{
    color: red;
    }
```

Using the "p,a" selector, both the paragraph and anchor elements will be rendered using red text. When reading a CSS rule literally, commas translate to AND. However, writing the CSS this way will result in all the text—even the unordered list—being red, which is not what you want in this case.

Now, your next target will be to isolate the elements included in the unordered list and color these in blue with the CSS rules. Let's analyze the following code:

```
    <ul>
    <li> <p class="bold">Blue and Bold</
p> </li>
    <li> <p>Blue</p> </li>
    <li> <p>Blue</p> </li>
    <li> <p>Blue and Bold and Italic</p>
</li>
    <li> <p>Blue</p> </li>
    <li> <p>Blue</p> </li>
    <li> <p>Blue</p> </li>
    </ul>
```

In this example all of the <li> tags are said to be descendants of the parent unordered list element **descendents** <ul>. This is because they appear within the unordered list element surrounded by <ul> and </ul>. In CSS, a selector is called the **descendant** of another element if it is contained within that element, at any level. Conversely, a selector is known as the **ancestor** of those elements which **ancestors** are contained within it. In the previous example, the unordered list elements are the ancestors of the elements found between the <ul> tags. If there is only one layer of differentiation, it becomes a parent-child relationship as well as the ancestor-descendant relationship. For example, consider the following:

**parent**

```
<li> <p>Blue and Bold</p> </li>
```

Here, the <li> element is the **parent** of the paragraph element, and the paragraph element is conversely the **child** of the <li> element.

**child**

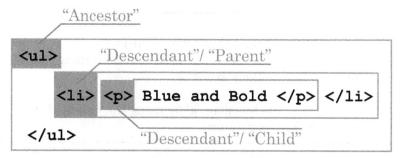

<ul> is the "ancestor" of <li>. <li> is the "Descendant" of <ul> and the "Parent" of <p>. <p> is the "Descendant" of <ul> and the "Child" of <li>.

With this understanding of the ancestor/descendent relationship, let's discuss the descendant selection rule which will be applied to all paragraph elements within the unordered list. The descendant selection rule takes a string of elements as input, where the first element should be the ancestor of all elements that follow. For example:

```
<head>
<style type="text/css">

p,a{
        color: red;
    }
ul p{
        color: blue;
      }
</style>
```

Here, the descendant selection rule is applied to all paragraph elements which have the unordered list <ul> as their ancestor. According to the CSS written, these will be colored blue.

If the unordered list contains more than the just paragraph elements, rather than writing new rules for all of those elements or creating a lengthy list separated by commas, you can write the following:

```
ul *{
          color: blue;
     }
```

Here, the * operator literally translates to 'everything', so this new rule applies to everything that has <ul> as their ancestor.

You can also make this rule less general by using the parent-child relationship in the following manner:

```
li > p{
          color: blue;
     }
```

This '>' sign represents a parent-child relationship, and signifies here that all paragraph elements which are the children of the li tag will appear blue.

Always remember that the descendant selection rules are more specific than the general CSS rules, and so they will have precedence. Hence, the previously red colored text under the unordered list will be overwritten in blue. The class selector, which we will discuss now, is more specific than the descendant selection rules.

Many different items on our page require bold and italic text. You can write a general CSS class rule for this purpose in the following way:

```
<head>
<style type="text/css">

p,a{
```

```
        color: red;
    }
li > p {
        color: blue;
        }
.bold{
        font-weight: bold;
        }
.ital{
        Font-style: italic;
        }
</style>
```

You can apply the class to individual HTML elements by using the class attribute within the HTML code itself. For example:

```
<body>
    <h1 class="ital">The Selectors Page
(This Text is Italic!)</h1>

    <p>Red</p>
    <p class="bold">Red and Bold</p>
    <a>Red</a>

    <ul>
        <li> <p class="bold">Blue and
Bold</p> </li>
        <li> <p>Blue</p> </li>
        <li> <p>Blue</p> </li>
        <li> <p class="bold ital">Blue and
Bold and Italic</p> </li>
        <li> <p>Blue</p> </li>
        <li> <p>Blue</p> </li>
        <li> <p>Blue</p> </li>
    </ul>
```

You can see that an element can have more than one CSS class applied to it. Here, you have to separate things with spaces, for example:

```
<li> <p class="bold   ital">Blue and Bold
and Italic</p> </li>
```

In order to color the last line of text on the page green, you can use the id selector (#). The id selector is different from the class selector in three ways. First, each id selector is only paired with a single element. Second, each element can have at most one id selector. And finally, id selectors are more specific than the class selector, so they definitely will get the highest priority in the cascade. Let's name our id selector *special* and use it in the following way:

```
<style type="text/css">

p,a{
      color: red;
    }
li > p {
          color: blue;
        }
.bold{
          font-weight: bold;
        }
.ital{
          font-style: italic;
        }
#special{
          color: green;
        }

</style>
```

In the HTML portion of the code, write the following:

```
    <p id="special">This text is Green,
usually.</p>
```

If you want the text purple when you move the mouse pointer over the element displayed in the browser, you can write the following code within the style tags:

```
#special:hover{
                color: purple;
        }
```

Hover is used as a pseudo-selector in this case because it modifies the selector #special. There are several uses for pseudo-selectors within CSS that we'll discuss later in the book.

Now that you understand selectors, you're well on your way to understanding how CSS works.

# 1.4 The 3 Ways to Deploy CSS

There are three ways to add CSS to your web page: inline, within a style tag or in-file block method, and in a separate CSS file. In this section all three methods are explained and how they interact when used on the same page is discussed.

**Adding CSS:**

1. Inline
2. Style Tags/ In-File Blocks
3. Separate CSS File

You should already be familiar with the in-file block method of CSS insertion, where a style tag is added to the page head. Any CSS rules that are declared within the style tag will be automatically applied. For instance:

```
<!DOCTYPE html>
<html>

<head>
<style type="text/css">
    p{
        color: red;
    }

</style>
</head>
```

Most websites are comprised of more than one HTML page, and sometimes you will want to apply the same style sheet to all or many of these pages. In this case, the in-file block method is weak, because it allows you to style only one page at a time, and you will have to copy large blocks of CSS into the headers of all of your pages.

If you use the in-line block style of inserting your CSS, you will also have difficulty maintaining your pages as you will have to make changes and edits in multiple CSS files to make global changes.

When you want to write a style sheet that will be applied to multiple HTML pages, it is generally a good idea to put that style sheet in a separate .css file. Let's consider the following example:

```
<!DOCTYPE html>
<html>

<head>
<link rel="stylesheet" type="text/css"
href="3ways.css" />

<style type="text/css">
   p{
        color: red;
      }

</style>
</head>
```

Here, above the style tag, there is a link element that has three values. The link element is telling the browser that you are linking to a style sheet and what type of style sheet you are using. The href value tells the browser where to look for the actual style sheet file. Here, the 3ways.css file is in the same folder as the HTML file. If your style sheets are in a separate folder, then you have to provide the exact path of that folder.

Let's take a look at the .css file itself. As is the case with the .html file, it will be written in a text editor, and the extension of the file will be .css. There is no special syntax associated with the CSS file. All you need to do is to start writing the CSS code, and the HTML pages that are linked to it will automatically use the CSS rules.

Consider the following HTML code:

```
<!DOCTYPE html>
<html>
<head>
<link rel="stylesheet" type="text/css"
href="3ways.css" />
<style type="text/css">

</style>
```

```
    </head>

    <body>
        <h1>Three ways to employ CSS</h1>

        <p>Separate File</p>
        <p>In-File Block</p>
        <p>In-Line</p>
    </body>
    </html>
```

The result will appear like this in the browser:

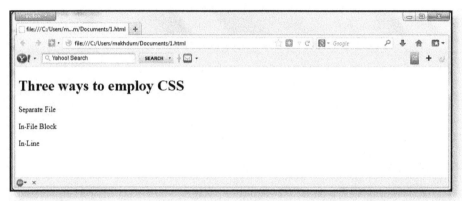

Figure 1.10: The browser view where there is a simple header element and paragraph elements.

Next, we'll create the external CSS file. There is no special type of syntax accompanying this file. In the text editor, you can simply write the following CSS code—defining all the paragraph elements will be blue—and save the file with the name 3ways.css in the same folder where the HTML file is:

```
p{
    color: blue;
}
```

Here, we have declared that all paragraph elements will be blue. In the browser, you will find the following:

**Figure 1.11:** The paragraph elements are colored in blue.

Now the question is, how does the web browser determine whether to give priority to the rules in our external CSS or the in-file block CSS? To determine this, you have to use both methods. In the HTML file, declare the rule in the following way:

```
<!DOCTYPE html>
<html>
<head>
<link rel="stylesheet" type="text/css"
href="3ways.css" />
<style type="text/css">
      p{
    color:red;
         }

</style>
</head>
```

In the browser, you will observe the following:

Figure 1.12: Red paragraph elements.

This shows that, despite the existence of the external CSS file, the web browsers give priority to the in-file block rule (which is described in the style element), since it is defined after the external CSS file rule. Although both the rules are equally specific, CSS always gives priority to the rule defined last.

If you want a specific paragraph element to be blue, you will have to make sure that there is a more specific selector, and you can use the class selector. In the CSS file, you can write the following:

```
.ex{
        color: blue;
    }
```

And modify the HTML file by writing:

```
<body>
    <h1>Three ways to employ CSS</h1>

    <p class="ex"> Separate File</p>
    <p>In-File Block</p>
    <p>In-Line</p>
</body>
</html>
```

Then the result will be:

**Figure 1.13:** Notice that the paragraph elements are colored in a different manner, where a specific class selector is used.

Now that you are familiar with the interaction between the separate CSS file and the in-file block CSS, let's look at the inline CSS. In order to make the last paragraph element both green and bold-faced, write the following in the HTML code:

```
<body>
    <h1>Three ways to employ CSS</h1>

    <p class="ex"> Separate File</p>
    <p>In-File Block</p>
    <p style="color: green; font-weight:
bold;">In-Line</p>

</body>
</html>
```

The result will be the following:

Figure 1.14: The browser view where you can see the three colored paragraph elements, where one of them is bold-faced.

What is achieved here through inline selectors can also be achieved, in general, through id selectors, so using inline CSS may seem to be extraneous and cluttering. However, it's very important to realize that inline CSS takes priority over all other CSS rules, with one distinctive exception. Using an 'important' flag, you can circumvent the styles. If you write this in the HTML code:

```
<style type="text/css">
p{
color: red !important;
  }
</style>
```

You will see that all the text will be colored red, despite the presence of external and Inline CSS. The 'important' flag will have the highest priority.

> Tip: While inline CSS seems convenient, most experts will tell you to avoid using it. Well-developed web and mobile sites separate the content (HTML) from the design (CSS). This allows for easier maintenance and content reuse. If you have CSS embedded in your content it is more difficult to display the content in other media.

In this section, you have learned the three separate methods of adding CSS to a document, and you learned how web pages determine which CSS rules get priority when the systems are used in synchrony.

# 1.5 INTRODUCING CSS3

As you already know, CSS is in a transitional period of its life cycle. CSS2, which we have been using for many years, is being phased out for the new version, CSS3. Because web browsers have to implement the new CSS3 rules, it would be very difficult for them if we switch from CSS2 to CSS3 all at once. So, the World Wide Web Consortium (W3C) is releasing CSS3 in a series of modules, small sections of the whole that will be adopted one at a time as standard CSS.

> **NOTE:** While CSS3 represents many significant upgrades and improvements over CSS2, much remains untouched. Your CSS2 knowledge will not go to waste as much of CSS2 code is common to the new version.

Take a look at the webpage www.w3.org/style/css/current-work.

You have to keep an eye on this site if you are doing a lot of CSS development, because these are the folks who decide how CSS3 is going to be implemented in standards-compliant browsers. This page has a list of the most current specifications. A small handful of CSS3 modules have been added to their recommended list, like CSS colors, namespaces and selectors. This means that they are supported by all major web browsers right now.

Most of the modules have the status "WD" or "Working Draft" (as shown in the following figure), which means that they have not yet been officially added to the list of CSS features that the web browsers must support to stay relevant. However, that does not mean that some web browsers have not already implemented these features to some degree. In this section, we will access one of these features which technically is still not part of the official W3C specification.

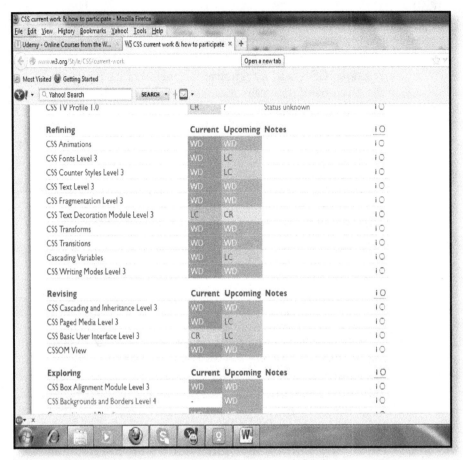

Figure 1.15 The currently recommended CSS3 rules as defined at www.w3.org.

Let us consider the following simple HTML code. It has a header and a 'div' element, which we'll describe shortly.

```
<!DOCTYPE html>
<html>
<head>
    <link rel="stylesheet" type="text/css"
href="css3_begin.css" />
</head>

<body>
    <h1>This page uses CSS3!</h1>
```

```
        <div id="rotated-div"></div>

</body>
</html>
```

In the external CSS file, the element 'div' is described in the following way:

```
#rotated-div{
    width: 400px;
    height: 400px;
    background-color: blue;

    /*IE 9*/
    /*Safari and Google Chrome*/
    /*Opera*/
    /*Mozilla Firefox*/
}
```

Viewed in the browser, the page looks like this:

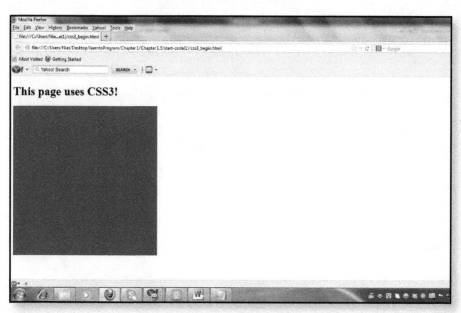

**Figure 1.16:** The browser view where a blue square is displayed.

One of the CSS3 modules which has not yet been added to the W3C recommended list is the 'transform' module. Using this module we can do something that we are not able to do with CSS2: rotate the 'div' element. The syntax to rotate the div looks like this (in the CSS file):

```
#rotated-div{
    width: 400px;
    height: 400px;
    background-color: blue;

    transform: rotate(45deg);
              }
```

If we were to load the page in the browser at this point nothing would happen. Although all of the major desktop web browsers have already implemented this transform-rotate functionality, they will not allow us to use this functionality directly since it is not yet included in the recommended list of W3C. So, we need to use a special syntax to use this functionality in the CSS file, as shown here:

```
#rotated-div{
   width: 400px;
   height: 400px;
   background-color: blue;

   transform: rotate(45deg);
   -ms-transform: rotate(45deg); /*IE 9*/
   -webkit-transform: rotate(45deg);
/*Safari and Google Chrome*/
   -o-transform: rotate(45deg); /*Opera*/
   -moz-transform: rotate(45deg); /*Mozilla
Firefox*/
          }
```

As a developer, you are signing an implicit contract with the web browsers that you are using this feature experimentally and the web browsers will not be held responsible if anything goes wrong. As you can see, the rule is similar for all the major web browsers. The result in the web browser will be the following:

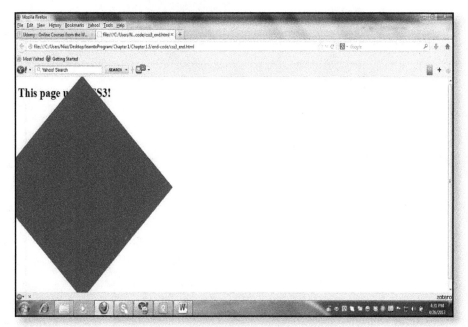

Figure 1.17: The 45°-rotated square element displayed in the browser.

Here the div element has been rotated 45°. This is something that we could not do with CSS2.

There are a lot of really exciting features expected to be implemented in CSS3, and we can access many of them already in this manner. Some of the really visually thrilling options with CSS3 are custom fonts, automated rounded borders and rudimentary animations. These are things that the CSS developers have been requesting for years.

Even if you are developing for an environment where it may not be appropriate to use these 'not-yet-recommended' features, it is a good idea to play around and familiarize yourself with the CSS3 options as you are exposed to them. Eventually, these modules will become recommended, and already by using these modules, web developers are making more visually appealing and exciting websites. So, try to be a little more adventurous right now, otherwise you might miss something really special.

# CHAPTER 1 LAB EXERCISE

Consider the following HTML code:

```
<!DOCTYPE html>
<html>
<head>
</head>

<body>
    <div>
        <h2>This Text is Red</h2>
        <p>This Text is usually Green, but
turns purple when we hover over it.</p>
        <p>This Text is Green</p>
        <p>This Text is Green</p>
    </div>
    <div>
        <h1>This Text is Green</h1>
        <p>This text is Red</p>
        <p>This text is Red</p>
        <p>This text is Red</p>
    </div>
</body>
</html>
```

Now, create a new .css file and modify the HTML code to use it. Style all the text on the page so that it is not bold.

Apply the opposite CSS rule (all text on the page IS bold) using the in-file method of CSS insertion. Be sure to place your new <style> tag after the existing <link> tag. Which rule takes precedence?

Move the <link> tag so that it now comes after the <style> tag in the page header (do not do this in real projects– it may confuse other developers). Now which rule manifests on the page?

Write CSS rules in the external file so that the page text is the color it

*CSS Development (with CSS3!)*

describes itself to be.

Order the rules in your CSS so that the rules that CSS gives the most weight are at the top of the page.

Use a descendant selector and the * (all) operator to select all elements who are the descendants of the <body> tag. Change the color of these elements back to black. Which elements resist this change?

Modify the previous rule with the *!important* flag so that ALL text on the page is black.

## QUESTIONS FOR REVIEW

1. Which web development technology can be used to make a website more visually appealing?
   a. HTML
   b. CSS
   c. Javascript
   d. PHP

2. Which of the following is correctly defined as a valid rgb style?
   a. rgb(0,255)
   b. rgb(255)
   c. rgb(255,0,255)
   d. rgb(0,0,0,255)

3. Which of the following is not a proper way to deploy CSS on a HTML page?
   a. Inline
   b. In-file Block
   c. In-child
   d. External CSS File

4. Which is the latest version of CSS as approved by W3C?
   a. CSS2
   b. CSS3
   c. CSS4
   d. CSS5

# CHAPTER 1 SUMMARY

In this chapter we learned about CSS and how it is used to style HTML pages. We learned how to color the text and the background of a webpage to make it aesthetically pleasing.

We discussed the proper use of CSS selectors, the different methods of adding CSS to the webpages, and how CSS prioritizes different rules to employ CSS in webpages.

In the next chapter, we will learn how to style text elements, tables, lists, backgrounds, and how to efficiently create drop-down menus.

# CHAPTER 2

## STYLING SPECIFIC ELEMENTS

### CHAPTER OBJECTIVES

- You will learn how to effectively style the text elements on a page using CSS.
- You will be able to understand how to change the background colors of your tables.
- You will know the way to use different kinds of bullets for your ordered and unordered lists.
- You will learn useful tips and tricks when it comes to designing the background of your webpage.
- You will understand the way to style a button using the sliding door technique.
- You will learn how to work with sprite sheets to display images one at a time in an appropriately-sized window.

## 2.1 STYLING TEXT ELEMENTS

In this section, we will be exploring the text styling options available to us in CSS. In order to do this, we will be styling two HTML pages. The first page presents a poem, and the second one presents a short story. Both pages are displayed in a very similar manner. We will be writing all of our CSS code in an external file, so that we do not have to write the rules twice that we are going to use for both the pages. Let's first look at the poetry page in the web browser:

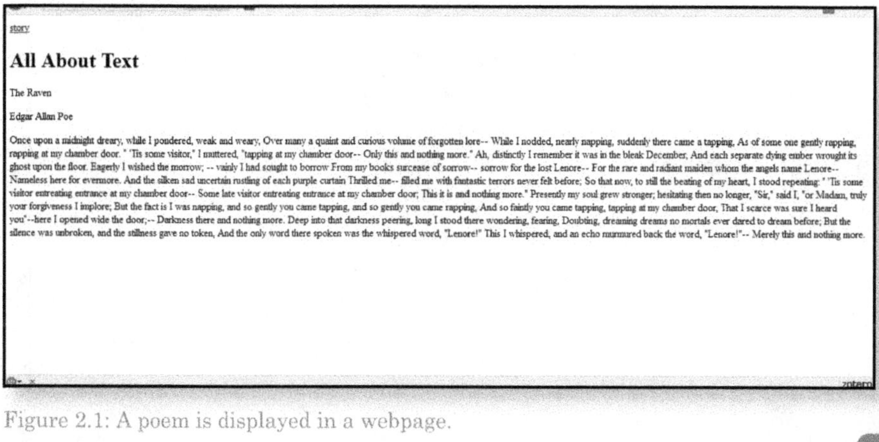

Figure 2.1: A poem is displayed in a webpage.

This is a very simple page that contains a header element, some paragraph elements and also a link to the 'story' page. The glaring issue is that our poem has been compressed into this big block of text, which does not look good. If we look at the corresponding HTML code, we will find the following:

## CODE LISTING: POEM PAGE HTML

```
<!DOCTYPE html>
<html>
<head>
    <link rel="stylesheet" type="text/css"
href="text_begin.css" />
</head>

<body>
    <a href="the_field_bazaar_begin.html"> story
</a>

    <h1>All About Text</h1>

    <p>The Raven</p>

    <p>Edgar Allan Poe</p>

    <p>
        Once upon a midnight dreary, while I
pondered, weak and weary,
        Over many a quaint and curious volume
of forgotten lore--
        While I nodded, nearly napping,
suddenly there came a tapping,
        As of someone gently rapping, rapping
at my chamber door.
        " 'Tis some visitor," I muttered,
"tapping at my chamber door--
        Only this and nothing more."

        Ah, distinctly I remember it was in
the bleak December,
```

And each separate dying ember wrought
its ghost upon the floor.
Eagerly I wished the morrow; -- vainly
I had sought to borrow
From my books surcease of sorrow--
sorrow for the lost Lenore--
For the rare and radiant maiden whom
the angels name Lenore--
Nameless here for evermore.

And the silken sad uncertain rustling
of each purple curtain
Thrilled me-- filled me with fantastic
terrors never felt before;
So that now, to still the beating of
my heart, I stood repeating:
" 'Tis some visitor entreating
entrance at my chamber door--
Some late visitor entreating entrance
at my chamber door;
This it is and nothing more."

Presently my soul grew stronger;
hesitating then no longer,
"Sir," said I, "or Madam, truly your
forgiveness I implore;
But the fact is I was napping, and so gently
you came tapping, and so    gently you came
rapping,
And so faintly you came tapping,
tapping at my chamber door,
That I scarce was sure I heard you"--
here I opened wide the door;--
Darkness there and nothing more.

Deep into that darkness peering, long
I stood there wondering, fearing,
Doubting, dreaming dreams no mortals
ever dared to dream before;
But the silence was unbroken, and the
stillness gave no token,

```
             And the only word there spoken was the
     whispered word, "Lenore!"
             This I whispered, and an echo murmured
     back the word, "Lenore!"--
             Merely this and nothing more.


     </p>

</body>
</html>
```

Here in this HTML code, you can see that the poem is presented in a much more readable manner, but when we go from HTML to browser display, some readability is lost. The issue is a CSS styling property called **white-space**.

 This *white-space* property is responsible for two related things. First, it describes how the text will handle the presence of spaces, tabs and new lines, what we call *white-space* as a whole. Secondly, it describes how the text will react if the space is given to it.

To begin playing with the *white-space* attribute, let's create the following class for the poem paragraph in the HTML code:

```
<p class="poem" >
Once upon a midnight.........
```

In the external CSS file, we can write the default *white-space* rule in the following way:

```
.poem{
    white-space: normal;
        }
```

This **normal** white-space rule declares two things. First, it declares that all white space collapses into a single space. Second, it declares that the text will wrap. The first one signifies that we will never see the new lines—we will only see the length of the white space equal to the length of a standard space bar space. That's what is bothering us with the display of the poem in the browser. We definitely need new lines to make our poem display as a poem should be displayed. **Wrapping** means that the text will add new lines when it comes to the end of its containing element. We can see this by shrinking the size of our window, thus compressing the width of the paragraph element that contains the text. The text adds new lines at the end of words so that it still displays properly in the width given to it, as shown in the following figure:

Figure 2.2: The poem is displayed in a shrunken window.

Now, instead of using the default *normal* rule for the purpose of white space, we have five more options. For instance, we can use the **nowrap** option in the following way:

```
.poem{
    White-space: nowrap;
    }
```

This is just like the *normal* rule mentioned previously, except for the fact that no wrapping will occur. This means that when we resize the browser window, rather than adding new lines to attempt to make the text fit, our browser will

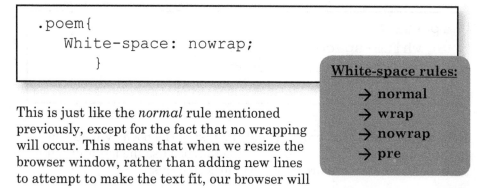

White-space rules:
→ normal
→ wrap
→ nowrap
→ pre

simply display whatever bit of text fits in our new frame of view, like this:

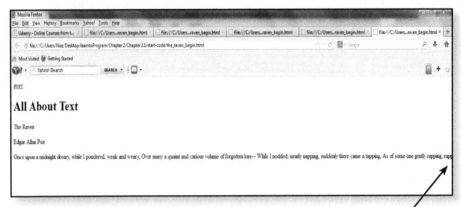

Figure 2.3: The poem is displayed in the page when no wrapping occurs.

Text runs past the window

However, this is not what we're looking for—we are interested in getting rid of the collapsing white-space property, while the property *nowrap* preserves it. Here, for this purpose, we can use the **pre**, or *preserve* option, in the following manner:

```
.poem{
    white-space: pre;
        }
```

If we want both to preserve white space and have some text wrapping, then we can choose both *pre-wrap* and *pre-line*. Here, we will use the *pre* property, because we do not want the browser to decide to break the lines of the poem. However, to ensure that our poem will really look like a poem in the browser, we should use **text-align** styling, as shown here:

```
.poem{
    white-space: pre;
        Text-align: center;
        }
```

Here we are telling the browser that the text of the poem will be aligned in the center. In a similar manner, we could also use the left and right alignment. Now, in the browser it will look like this:

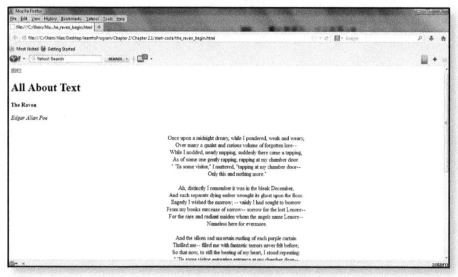

Figure 2.4: The poem displayed, appropriately styled, in the browser.

This is what we were looking for, the most preferable format for a poem. Now, let's do some aesthetic styling. If you want to underline the h1 element to separate it from the rest of the page, write the following in the CSS file:

```
h1{
    text-decoration: underline;
    }
```

In the browser, you will find:

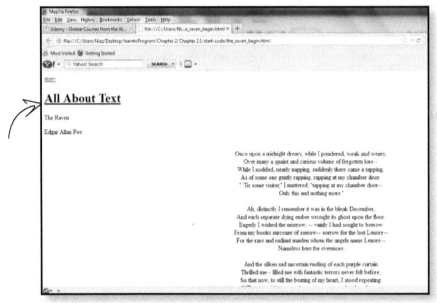

Figure 2.5: The header element is underlined.

The other options for text decoration are **overline**, where the line appears over the text, and **line-through**, where the line appears through the text.

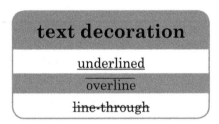

Next we are going to look at our 'short story' page. In the HTML file, you can put the following:

## CODE LISTING: STORY PAGE HTML

```
<!DOCTYPE html>
<html>
<head>
    <link rel="stylesheet" type="text/css"
href="text_begin.css" />
```

```
</head>

<body>
    <a href="the_raven_begin.html"> poem </a>

    <h1>All About Text</h1>

    <p>The Field Bazaar</p>

    <p>Sir Arthur Conan Doyle</p>

    <p>
        "I Should certainly do it," said
Sherlock Holmes.
        I started at the interruption, for my
companion had been eating his breakfast with
his attention entirely centered upon the paper
which was propped up by the coffee pot.  Now I
looked across at him to find his eyes fastened
upon me with the half-amused, half-questioning
expression which he usually assumed when he
felt he had made an intellectual point.
        "Do what?" I asked.
        He smiled as he took his slipper from
the mantelpiece and drew from it enough shag
tobacco to fill the old clay pipe with which he
invariably rounded off his breakfast.
        "A most characteristic question of
yours, Watson," said he.  "You will not, I am
sure, be offended if I say that any reputation
for sharpness which I may possess has been
entirely gained by the admirable foil which
you have made for me.  Have I not heard of
debutantes who have insisted upon plainness in
their chaperones?  There is a certain analogy."
        Our long companionship in the Baker
Street rooms had left us on those easy terms of
intimacy when much may be said without offence.
And yet I acknowledged that I was nettled at
his remark.
        "I may be very obtuse," said I, "but
```

I confess that I am unable to see how you have managed to know that I was... I was..."

"Asked to help in the Edinburgh University Bazaar..."

"Precisely. The letter has only just come to hand, and I have not spoken to you since."

"In spite of that," said Holmes, leaning back in his chair and putting his finger tips together, "I would even venture to suggest that the object of the bazaar is to enlarge the University cricket field."

I looked at him in such bewilderment that he vibrated with silent laughter.

"The fact is, my dear Watson, that you are an excellent subject," said he. "You are never blase. You respond instantly to any external stimulus. Your mental processes may be slow but they are never obscure, and I found during breakfast that you were easier reading than the leader in the Times in front of me."

"I should be glad to know how your arrived at your conclusions," said I.

"I fear that my good nature in giving explanations has seriously compromised my reputation," said Holmes. "But in this case the train of reasoning is based upon such obvious facts that no credit can be claimed for it. You entered the room with a thoughtful expression, the expression of a man who is debating some point in his mind. In your hand you held a solitary letter. Now last night you retired in the best of spirits, so it was clear that it was this letter in your hand which had caused the change in you."

"This is obvious."

"It is all obvious when it is explained to you. I naturally asked myself what the letter could contain which might have this affect upon you. As you walked you held the flap side of the envelope towards me, and I saw upon it the same shield-shaped device which I have observed upon your old college cricket cap. It was clear, then, that the request came from Edinburgh University - or from some club connected with the University. When you reached the table you laid down the letter beside your plate with the address uppermost, and you walked over to look at the framed photograph upon the left of the mantelpiece."

It amazed me to see the accuracy with which he had observed my movements. "What next?" I asked.

"I began by glancing at the address, and I could tell, even at the distance of six feet, that it was an unofficial communication. This I gathered from the use of the word 'Doctor' upon the address, to which, as a Bachelor of Medicine, you have no legal claim. I knew that University officials are pedantic in their correct use of titles, and I was thus enabled to say with certainty that your letter was unofficial. When on your return to the table you turned over your letter and allowed me to perceive that the enclosure was a printed one, the idea of a bazaar first occurred to me. I had already weighed the possibility of its being a political communication, but this seemed improbable in the present stagnant conditions of politics.

```
    </p>
</body>
</html>
```

In the browser, you will see the following:

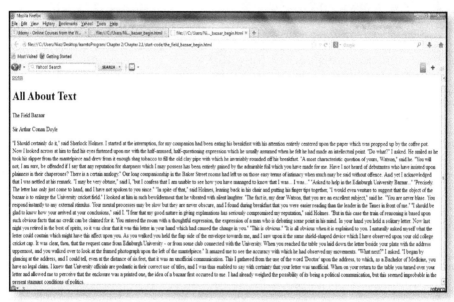

Figure 2.6: The short story is displayed in the webpage.

Now, if you want to do some custom styling in the story and poem titles, you can declare separate classes to differentiate them from other paragraph elements in the following way:

```
<p class="title">The Raven</p>
<p class="author">Edgar Allan Poe</p>
```

You can do the same thing for the story page. In the CSS file, you can make all the titles bold-faced text, and make the author element italic, as shown here:

```
.title{
    font-weight: bold;
}

.author{
    font-style: italic;
}
```

*CSS Development (with CSS3!)*

Have a look at the browser:

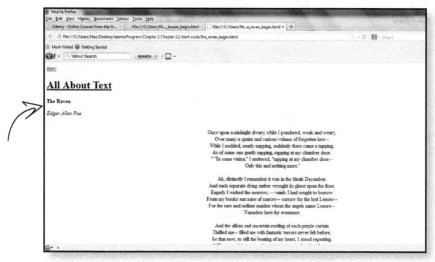

Figure 2.7: The underlined, bold-faced and italicized text for the poem page.

You can also do some interesting things with the hyperlink text because hyperlink has a few different states, such as *mouse-over* and *clicked*. In the HTML page, the hyperlink is included as an anchor element in the following way:

```
<a href="the_field_bazaar_begin.html"> story
</a>
```

You can style this element in the CSS file using the following code:

```
a:link{
    color: #ffffff;   /* white */
}
a:visited{
    color: #ffffff;
}
a:hover{
    color: #0000ff;   /* blue */
}
a:active{
    color: #00ff00;   /* lime */
}
```

In order to make these links on our page invisible to the casual observer, you can turn this link white, as is done here. However, when you put the mouse over it, it turns blue, and when you click it, it turns green. Always remember that you can only use the *hover* pseudo selector if you have already used the *link* and *visited* pseudo selectors for that element. You can also use the *active* pseudo selector if you have already used the *link*, *visited* and *hover* pseudo selectors for the element.

**Link Elements:**
→ link
→ visited
→ hover
→ active

Now it's time to style our story page. In the CSS file, add the following code:

```
.story{
    white-space: pre-wrap;
    font-family: "Arial", sans-serif;
        }
```

Here, you can see that instead of the option *pre* or *preserve* that we have chosen for handling the *white-space* property for the poem, here we have used *pre-wrap*, because we want wrapping to occur. We did not use the *pre-line* option, because that would remove any tabs that the author added in the story. Moreover, we have also changed the font that our story is presented in. In CSS2 we did that with the *font-family* property. Here, we have used the arial font. An important thing to understand regarding fonts when it comes to CSS2 is that a browser can only display the fonts that are loaded on the machine it's running on. Although arial is a web-safe font and it should be loaded on any machine viewing webpages, this cannot be guaranteed. So, we can specify backup fonts by separating the fonts with commas. Here, we have specified a sans-serif font as the backup. However, sans-serif is not a font, it's a family of fonts, and the machine knows this. So if the arial font is unavailable, the machine will use any font belonging to the family of sans-serif.

**List of web-safe fonts:**
http://www.w3schools.com/cssref/css_websafe_fonts.asp

Our last task is to modify the font that our poem appears in. However, we will not use a web-safe font here. Instead, we will use a Google Font which we will download from Google's website. Add this stylesheet link to your HTML file just after the *<head>* tag. (This should be the first line of the *<head></head>* section.) This link will request the *Tangerine* font from Google's website.

```
<link rel="stylesheet" type="text/
css" href="http://fonts.googleapis.com/
css?family=Tangerine">
```

In the CSS file, we now instruct the web browser to use the *Tangerine* font which we downloaded.

```
.poem{
    white-space: pre;
    text-align: center;
    font-family: tangerine;
    font-size: 32px;
    font-weight: bold;
}
```

Now, when you look in the browser, you will find the following:

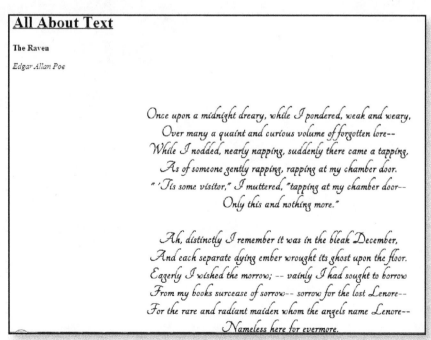

Figure 2.8: The poem presented in the webpage with a beautiful font.

In this section, you have learned the concepts of white-space preservation, wrapping, the way to style links in various states, and how to create bold, italic and underlined fonts, and you have an understanding of how fonts are handled as a whole by the web browser and the CSS.

 QUESTIONS FOR REVIEW

1. The property to effectively handle the presence of spaces, tabs and new lines is called what?
   a. White-space property.
   b. Black-space property.
   c. White-tabs property.
   d. Black-tabs property.

2. Which rule is used to make sure that when we put our mouse over the menu, something will be displayed?
   a. click.
   b. hover.
   c. push.
   d. apply.

# 2.2 STYLING TABLES AND LISTS

In this section we will explore the basic options available to us when styling tables and lists in CSS. We will be modifying the following page, where there is a single table, containing four lists and some basic text:

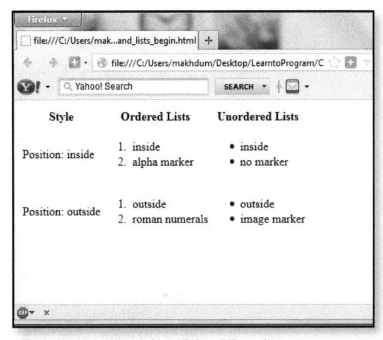

Figure 2.9: The webpage showing a table with four different lists.

The corresponding HTML code is given here:

## CODE LISTING: STYLING TABLES HTML

```
<!DOCTYPE html>
<html>
<head>
    <link rel="stylesheet" type="text/css"
href="tables_and_lists_begin.css" />
</head>

<body>
    <table id="list_table">
        <tr>
```

```
                <th>Style</th>
                <th>Ordered Lists</th>
                <th>Unordered Lists</th>
        </tr>
        <tr>
                <td>Position: inside</td>
                <td>
                        <ol id="ol_1">
                                <li>inside</li>
                                <li>alpha marker</li>
                        </ol>
                </td>
                <td>
                        <ul id="ul_1">
                                <li>inside</li>
                                <li>no marker</li>
                        </ul>
                </td>
        </tr>
        <tr>
                <td>Position: outside</td>
                <td>
                        <ol id="ol_2">
                                <li>outside</li>
                                <li>roman numerals</
li>
                        </ol>
                </td>
                <td>
                        <ul id="ul_2">
                                <li>outside</li>
                                <li>image marker</li>
                        </ul>
                </td>
        </tr>
    </table>
</body>
</html>
```

Let's make the table more aesthetically pleasing by modifying each of the list elements so that they all use slightly different settings.

We'll start by styling the table. The first thing we should do is to add a border to the table, because right now it seems that the elements are simply floating based on the white space. We do this in the external CSS file with the name *tables_and_lists_begin.css*:

```
#list_table{
        border: 1px solid black;
}
```

Here, we have defined the width of the border to be 1 pixel, and for the visual style of the border we have chosen the 'solid' option, which will give us a plain and simple border of a solid color. Let's choose black. If we take a look at the browser, you will find the following:

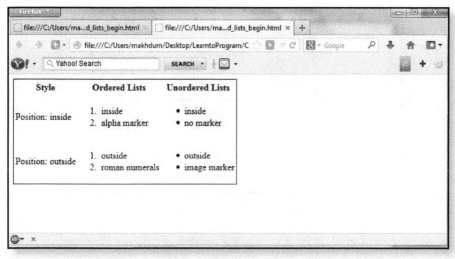

Figure 2.10: The table with a border around it

The table has a border now, but the individual cells of the table are still undefined, meaning they are not separated from each other. To do this, let's use the descendant selection rule to access both the table's header cells and the normal cells, in the following manner:

```
#list_table{
        border: 1px solid black;
}
```

```
#list_table th{
      border: 1px solid black;


}
#list_table td{
      border: 1px solid black;
}
```

Here, we wanted all of our table's borders to look the same, so we used the same rule for each case. In the browser, you will get the following:

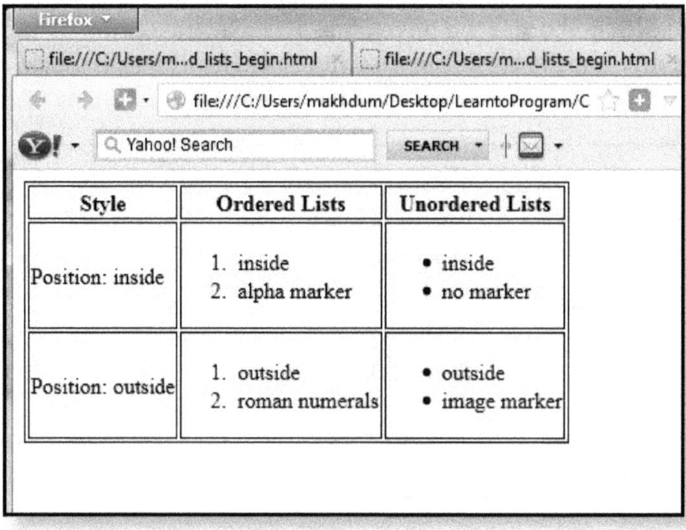

Figure 2.11: The table with a double border around each cell

You can see that each cell has a double border, while we were only expecting a single border. that's because each cell is getting its own border, regardless of the fact that the border of the other cells or the table as a whole may already exist. You can easily fix this problem by using the *border-collapse* option in the following way:

```
#list_table{
    border: 1px solid black;
    border-collapse: collapse;
}
```

In the browser, it will look like this:

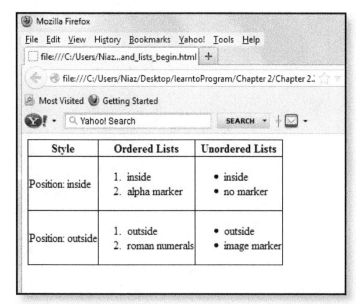

Figure 2.12: The double border is removed around each cell

Here with the border-collapse rule, we are telling the browser that whenever two borders are normally drawn in the same place, we want our table to drop one. In this way, we can get the borders as per our expectations.

Before we add color to our table, we can play a little bit with its bottom cells. You can see in our table that the words "roman numerals" and "image marker" are nearly touching the border, which does not look good at all. We can modify this using the rule *padding*, which defines the space between the element in the cell and its border. We can use this rule in the following manner:

```
#list_table td{
        border: 1px solid black;
        padding:10px;
    }
```

In the browser, the altered table will look like this:

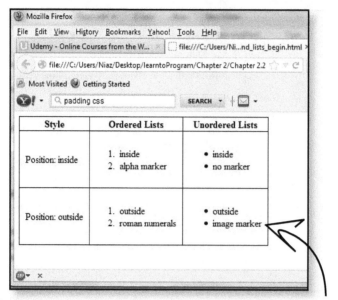

Figure 2.13: The space between the cell element and its border has increased.

Here, we have chosen 10 pixels as the mandatory degree of separation, and you can see that the cells in the table look much better.

Now, let's add some color to our table. Here in the CSS code you can notice that our general rule for tables is less specific than the rules for our header cells and general cells. This means that whatever we declare for our general table rule, it will simply act as a default until we update the value in either of these rules for our header and general cells. Next, let's set the default background color as light green, like this:

```
#list_table{
    border: 1px solid black;
    border-collapse: collapse;

    background-color: #33CC33;
}
```

In the rule where we defined the table headers, let's change the background color to a darker green, and change the color of the text within these cells to white. At the same time, you can change the color of all the borders to white as well, which will help the table blend into the white page, while still maintaining the dividers between the cells of the table. The entire code should be the following:

## CODE LISTING: STYLING TABLES CSS

```
#list_table{
border: 1px solid white;
border-collapse: collapse;

background-color: #33CC33;
}

#list_table th{
        border: 1px solid white;

        background-color: #004400;
        color: white;
    }
    #list_table td{
        border: 1px solid white;
        padding: 10px;
    }
```

In the browser, you will find the following:

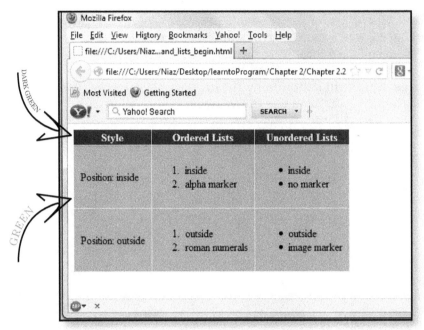

Figure 2.14: The table with colored background.

Now, let's style the lists of the table. The first list-styling rule that we are going to apply here is called *list-style-position*. This rule declares whether or not the markers of the list count as physical objects in terms of the list-positioning, wrapping, and interaction with all other elements. The markers, which are declared to be *outside*, don't have any physical interaction with anything. The default is the position *outside*, so in this sense our lists in the bottom of our table look nice, because they are according to our position *outside* rule. We just need to change the position rule of our top two lists. We can do this in the following way in the external CSS file:

```
#ol_1{
    list-style-position: inside;
}
#ul_1{
    list-style-position: inside;
}
```

Applying this code will move the corresponding markers from nonphysical elements, which just float to the left of the contents of the list, to physical elements that now must be wrapped in position around everything else. If we make the change, and look at the browser, we will see that our lists will move to the right, because now our markers are centered in the cell, rather than the text that came to the right of them, as in the following way:

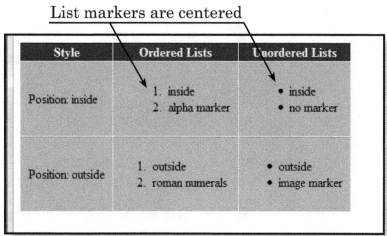

Figure 2.15: The markers in the top row are centered in the cell in the top row.

Now, we can change the type of the markers that we have used here. Let's start with the ordered lists. For the top ordered list, we are going to change the type of the markers from the standard numbers to the alphabetical values (A, B...). For the bottom ordered list, we are going to change from the decimal numbers to roman numerals. We can use the following code:

```
#ol_1{
    list-style-position: inside;
    list-style-type: upper-alpha;
}

#ol_2{
    list-style-type: upper-roman;
}
```

The result will look like this:

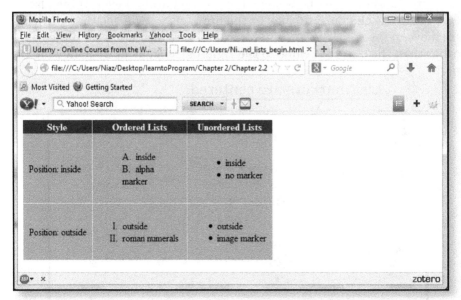

Figure 2.16: The type of markers in the ordered lists have been changed to alphabetical characters and roman numerals, respectively.

Here, we could also use *lower-alpha* and *lower-roman* instead of *upper-alpha* and *upper-roman*.

Our final step is to remove any marker for the top unordered list and to use a custom image as a marker for the bottom unordered list. To do this, we can use the following code:

**List Marker Styles:**

A. upper-alpha
b. lower-alpha
III. upper-roman
iv. lower-roman

```
#ul_1{
    list-style-position: inside;
    list-style-type: none;
}

#ul_2{
    list-style-image: url("picture.png");
}
```

This *picture.png* file should be in the same folder where the corresponding HTML and CSS file remain. Now, you will see the following in the browser:

*CSS Development (with CSS3!)*

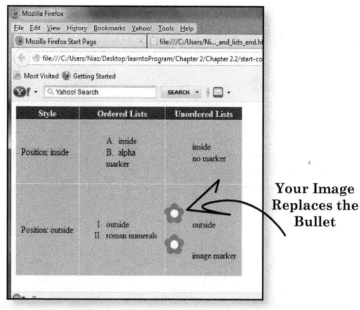

Figure 2.17: The type of markers in the unordered lists are changed to *no-markers* and *pictures*, respectively.

After following this chapter, you should have a lot of options available for styling tables and lists in CSS. It should also be noted that every rule mentioned in this chapter is specific to CSS2, not CSS3. You can also explore the other options available for styling tables and lists. There are many other styling options available for the markers of lists besides the things already mentioned here.

## QUESTIONS FOR REVIEW

1. What option do we use to remove the double border around each cell of a table to ensure that there is a single border ?
    a. border-merge          c. border-delete
    b. border-collapse      d. border-remove

2. Which of the following is the correct way to insert a picture as the bullet of the lists?
    a. list-style-image: url("picture.png");
    b. list-style-image: address("picture.png");
    c. list-style-image: source("picture.png");
    d. list-style-image: photo("picture.png");

## 2.3 STYLING BACKGROUNDS

In this section we are going to learn how CSS handles background images. First, we are going to add an image to the background of our page. In order to do that, create a folder named *images* in the same directory where your HTML and CSS files are located. Now, save any image in that folder with the name *full_bkg.png*. In the HTML file, write down the following code:

```
<!DOCTYPE html>
<html>
<head>
    <link rel="stylesheet" type="text/css"
href="backgrounds.css" />
</head>

<body class="main_body">
    <h1>The Backgrounds Page</h1>
</body>
</html>


In the external CSS file, in order to put
the image in the background, write the
following code:

.main_body{
    width: 1000px;
    height: 600px;
    background-image: url('images/full_bkg.
png');
}
```

In the browser, you will find the following:

Figure 2.18: A webpage with a nice background, where the image *Full_bkg.png* is used as the background image.

The actual image used for this background is actually larger than what the browser can display in its window. We can dynamically resize the background image using the *background-size* property, like this:

```
.main_body{
    width: 1000px;
    height: 600px;
    background-image: url('images/full_bkg.
jpg');
    background-size: 100% auto;
    -moz-background-size: 100% auto;
}
```

In the browser, you will see the following:

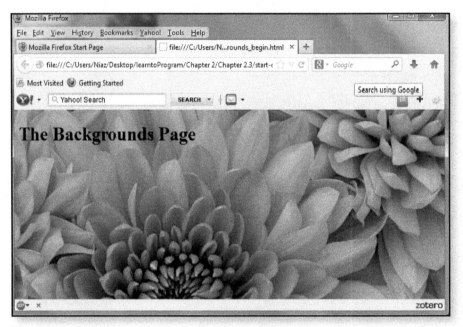

Figure 2.19: A webpage with a dynamically resized background image.

Now, let's analyze the code. The *background-size* rule is a rule particularly specific for CSS3. However, all major browsers support *background-size* in some level. The only thing that you should note is that for Mozilla Firefox, we have to use a specific syntax, which is shown in the code.

The *background-size* property takes two parameters: the width and the height for our new background. We can give these parameters in three different ways. We can simply say:

```
background-size: auto auto;
```

If we say this, the browser will simply use the default values and we will not get any change in the webpage. Instead of doing that, we can use pixel values in the following manner:

```
background-size: 1280px 780px;
```

The 1280 x 780 pixels is already the width and height of our background image, so again we cannot expect any change in the browser.

Widthwise, we want our background to stretch to fit the entire screen, and for that we can use a percentage value. However, if we write the code in this way:

```
background-size: 100% 100%;
```

Then we can see that the background looks very odd, because it will not be stretched vertically to the entire screen, rather it will only be as large as the header element it contains, as you can see here:

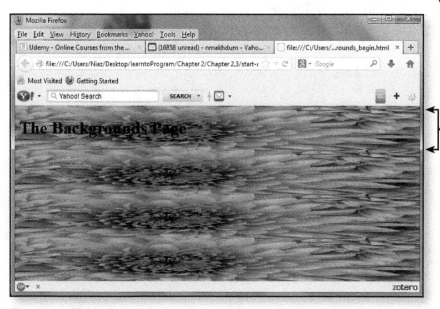

Figure 2.20: The background image is repeated vertically.

Here, the background gets shrunk, and then repeated vertically, which is certainly not what we are trying to do. So, we should use the automatic height in the following manner, and only then we will get the desired result:

```
background-size: 100% auto;
-moz-background-size: 100% auto;
```

Now we are going to add two background images to our webpage. Here, we want to put the image *partial_bkg* in the background, which is the picture of a tree, and located in the same folder where we are working. We also want to make sure that this picture is always visible no matter how the page is resized or scrolled. Our second background image is *gradient_bkg'* which is only a couple of pixels wide, but it has an interesting black-to-white shading, which will make the webpage look beautiful with a black-to-white effect. These two images are displayed here:

Figure 2.21: partial_bkg.png     Figure 2.22: gradient_bkg.png

In the CSS file, write the following:

```
.main_body{
    width: 1000px;
    height: 600px;
    background-image: url('images/partial_
bkg.png'), url('images/gradient_bkg.png');

}

h1{
    color: white;
    font-size: 50px;
}
```

CSS3 allows us to declare multiple background images for a single element. In this case, the two rules are both declared in the body element and separated by a comma. The image that we declare first will appear at the front of the other background image in the browser, where it will look like this:

*CSS Development (with CSS3!)*

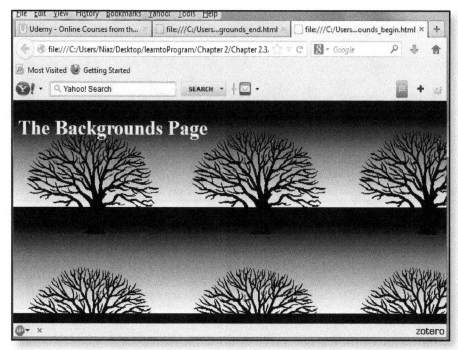

Figure 2.23: The webpage with two different background images, which are repeated.

Here we can see both of our background images, but we don't want our *gradient_bkg* image repeating vertically, and we also don't want the tree, or the *partial_bkg* image to repeat at all. We simply want this picture to be located at the bottom right-hand corner of our page. We can stop the repetition by using the following code:

> **Background Properties:**
> → repeat
> → no-repeat
> → repeat-x
> → repeat-y

```
.main_body{
    width: 1000px;
    height: 600px;
    background-image: url('images/partial_
bkg.png'), url('images/gradient_bkg.png');
    background-repeat: no-repeat, repeat-x;
    }
```

Here, in order to deal with repetition, we use the property *background-repeat*. For the first image where we don't want any repetition at all, we have used the *no-repeat* option. We want the second background image to be repeated along the x-axis, so we used the *repeat-x* option. If we wanted to repeat this image vertically, we could have written *repeat-y* instead. Now, in the browser, it will look like this:

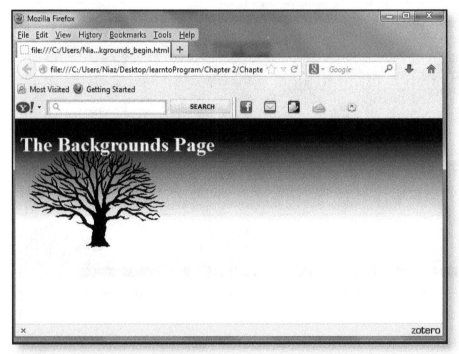

Figure 2.24: The background image showing the tree is displayed just once, and the other image is repeated only along the x-axis.

Next, we are going to put our *partial_bkg* image at the bottom right-hand corner of our page. We will use the *background-position* option, like this:

```
.main_body{
    width: 1000px;
    height: 600px;
    background-image: url('images/partial_
bkg.png'), url('images/gradient_bkg.png');

background-repeat: no-repeat, repeat-x;
    background-position: right bottom, left
top;
    }
```

Just like the *background-size* option that we have used earlier, we are going to specify the x-coordinate and the y-coordinate values for the *background-position* option. We can do this in terms of pixels or in terms of percentages, and also in terms of preset values which we are going to use now. Let's change the positioning of our first image, the *partial_bkg* one which is the image of a tree, to be *right bottom*, and then change the positioning of our second image to be *left top*, which is the default position. Here, we can also use the keyword *center*. In the browser, it will look like this:

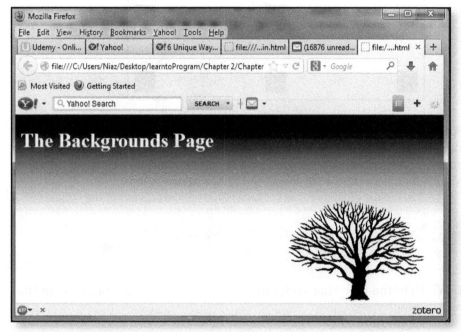

Figure 2.25: The background image showing the tree is displayed at the bottom-right corner.

**Tip:** If your browser doesn't produce a similar display as is shown in Figure 2.25, your display terminal may have a different resolution. In that case, you'll have to adjust the values of your *width* and *height* parameters in your CSS file.

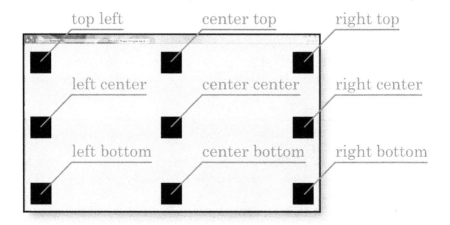

So, here is our uniquely styled webpage. At the end of this chapter, you should be totally comfortable with setting the background of your pages. The techniques that are covered here should serve nearly all your requirements related to styling the background.

 QUESTIONS FOR REVIEW

1. Which of the following styles in CSS is used to display an image in the background?
   a. background-image
   b. image-background
   c. background-photo
   b. photo-background

2. Which of the following allows us to declare multiple background images for a single element?
   a. CSS1
   b. CSS2
   c. CSS3
   d. None of the above

# 2.4 THE SLIDING-DOOR TECHNIQUE (MAKING A CSS BUTTON)

In this section we are going to style a button using pre-rendered images. In order to do this, we will have to utilize an advanced CSS rule, which can be called the **sliding door technique**. When we want to add images to HTML elements through CSS, a common scenario is that when the HTML element resizes, we want the images to be resized along with them. With the advent of CSS3, sometimes we can just stretch or compress our images according to the new HTML element's width or height. But oftentimes the stretched or compressed images do not look quite as we intended. In these instances, the sliding door technique can often be just what we need. This rule takes two or more images and attempts to display them so that they appear to be one image of any size.

Here we will use the sliding door technique in two images to create a button that can be almost any width. In reality, no button we create with this technique can be wider than the first image that we used, but if you think you might need very wide buttons, all you need to do is to extend the image to the right.

Our first image is displayed here:

Figure 2.26: button_normal_left.png

As you can see, it comprises more than two thirds of the button, including its left cap and center section. Our second image is given here, which has the third part, or the right cap of the button:

Figure 2.27: button_normal_right.png

If we look at the first image, we can see that the center section is much wider than we need it to be. So, if we insert the right cap in the middle part of this image, it will cut off the display of all the rest of the image afterwards. The right cap slides onto the image and locks it to a certain size, thus the name *sliding door technique.*

In order to apply the *sliding door technique*, we need to write the HTML code in the anchor element in a specific way, as shown here:

```
<!DOCTYPE html>
<html>
<head>
    <link rel="stylesheet" type="text/css"
href="button_begin.css" />
</head>

<body>
    <a class="button" href=#><span>Button</
span></a>
</body>
</html>
```

Right now, the only way for us to display both the right and left-hand sides of our button would be to assign the anchor elements as background images. That would allow us to display the images, but we would not be able to cut off the images when required. We are going to circumvent this issue by placing a *span* tag within the anchor element. This span tag would be the home of most of the button images. We will achieve the cut off effect because of the fact that logically this span element cannot be larger than the anchor element which contains it.

We are going to be styling two different elements: the *anchor* element with the class *button*, and also the *span* element that is contained in the *anchor* element. The CSS code that we are going to use is given here:

```
a.button{
    height: 30px;

    background-color: transparent;
    background-image: url("images/button_
normal_right.png");
    background-repeat: no-repeat;

    background-position: top right;
```

```
    float:left;
    display:block;

}

a.button span{
    background-color: transparent;
    background-image: url("images/button_
normal_left.png");

    line-height: 20px;
    display:block;

}
```

Let's analyze the code. The anchor element is going to be where we place the right-hand cap, and the span element is going to have most of our visible button, which is the left-hand cap along with the middle section. So, we have added the right-hand cap to our anchor element in the following manner:

```
a.button{
background-image: url("images/button_
normal_right.png");
}
```

As a precaution, we have changed the background color to transparent, by doing this:

```
background-color: transparent;
```

The reason for this is, by using a colored image file we have already declared a fixed color for this button, so we don't want any background color messing with the color of the button, and making the button appear as we did not intend it to.

We also wanted to make sure that the background does not repeat, so we have used the following:

```
background-repeat: no-repeat;
```

Right now, within the anchor element, the right-hand cap will be displayed on the left-hand side of the anchor element. We have fixed this by doing this:

```
background-position: top right;
```

Again, our button is not going to be resized vertically, it is only going to be resized horizontally. So, we have given it a mandatory height of 30 pixels, which is the height of the image file that we are using:

```
height: 30px;
```

We also want this element to be floating, because otherwise the top and bottom part of our images will not display outside of the text. We want our button to go around the text, so we have used the following rule:

```
float:left;
```

In order to display the button in 'block' form, we have used this code:

```
display:block;
```

Again, we have added the left-hand cap and the center portion of our button into our span element in the following manner:

```
a.button span{

background-image: url("images/button_
normal_left.png");

        }
```

To ensure that our text is positioned properly, we have assigned a fixed height for the line, like this:

```
line-height: 20px;
```

Let's take a look at it in the web browser:

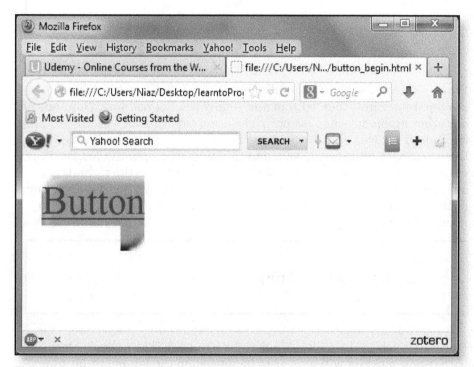

Figure 2.28: The webpage with a colored button

You can see that the button doesn't look very good. There are three issues relevant to our current button, and they can all be fixed with the **padding** rule. We want our right-hand cap to be displayed properly. Another problem is that the left side of the button is not visibly displaying down below where our text field is. The third thing that we want to do is to add padding to the left and right-hand sides so that the "Button" text does not push so close to the edges of the button.

Let's start by fixing the left side of the image. The reason why we are seeing a portion of the image on the left side is that the display area of the span is only as high as the line height that we declared. Our button is only 30 pixels high, so is the image that we are trying to display. So if we pad the span with 5 pixels on top and 5 pixels on the bottom, we can have

30 pixels of vertical display area for our image to look better. We can do that in this way:

```
a.button span{

background-image: url("images/button_
normal_left.png");
padding: 5px 0 5px 0;
    }
```

When we declare all of our padding in one line, then we are declaring the top, then right, then bottom and finally the left padding. Now, one of our other problems was that our right-hand cap was not actually capping the button—it was only stuck at the right of the left image. We can fix this issue with padding as well, and this time using *padding-right*. If we increase the display area of this anchor element to the right, then our image should display further to the right, because that is where our background is positioned. So, let's just increase the display area by 10 pixels, like this:

```
a.button{
padding-right: 10px;
}
```

Here, 10 pixels is the width of our right-hand cap. The only problem is that now our text will appear to be pushed to the left of our button, because the text will be rendering in the span. We can easily solve this problem by simply adding equal padding to the span on the left. In this way, we will be pushing the text away from both directions, and the text will appear right in the middle of our button. We can change the code in the following manner:

```
a.button span{

background-image: url("images/button_
normal_left.png");
padding: 5px 0 5px 10px;
    }
```

Here, we are not actually pushing the text—we are just resizing the button. Let's take a look at it in the browser:

Figure 2.29: The button with a beautiful shape.

This actually looks like a very reasonable button. The last thing we are going to do is assign a very rudimentary animation to the button, that will animate when we place our mouse over it. We will do it using the *hover* property, like this:

```
a.button:hover{
background-image:url("images/button_hover_
right.png");
}

a.button:hover span{
background-image: url("images/button_hover_
left.png");
}
```

Here we have used the following two similar types of images with different names:

Figure 2.30: button_hover_left.png

Figure 2.31: button_hover_right.png

The shadows on this button image are flipped. This will create the illusion that the button is being pushed in when applied as a *hover* property.

In this section you should have a clear idea about the concept behind the *sliding door technique* of creating a button. Even though CSS3 is reducing the number of cases where we need to use this sort of second-level technique, this *sliding door technique* coupled with images means that we can create a resizable object that looks like whatever we want, no matter what the functionality of CSS that we are using happens to be.

# QUESTIONS FOR REVIEW

1. Which rule takes two or more images and attempts to display them so that they appear to be one image of any size?
   a. sliding door technique.
   b. sliding window technique.
   c. merging door technique.
   d. merging window technique.

2. How can you ensure that the button is only resized horizontally?
   a. By giving it a manadatory height.
   b. By exclusively defining in which way it is going to be resized.
   c. It cannot be ensured.
   d. It will be automatically ensured.

# 2.5 Sprite Sheets and Images

This chapter will cover the **sprite sheets** in CSS. A *sprite sheet* is a single image which appears to contain multiple images.

For example, consider the following *sprite sheet*:

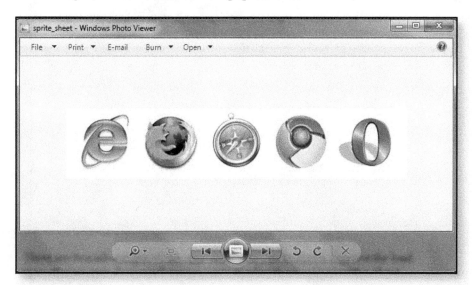

Figure 2.32: Sprite_sheet

This *sprite sheet* contains five distinct images, or five browser icons. We call each of these individual images sprites. The idea behind the *sprite sheet* is that we can get away with using the single image file for five different images by rendering only a portion of the sprite sheet when we would normally render one of these images in its entirety.

There are two advantages of this approach. First, *sprite sheets* improve the load time of your page, because there are some overheads associated with a client running a browser asking the server to send it an image. With today's modern high-speed internet connections, this is less important than it used to be, but in some instances where pages load many unique images, there can be a significant improvement. The other thing *sprite sheets* do is improve the organization of our webpage. These browser icons in the previous figure are all related images. So, rather than having five separate image files to load and manage in our HTML and CSS code, we can always load these as just one image and then navigate to the portion of the sprite sheet that we like to use.

In this chapter we are going to use this sprite sheet to create an HTML image object—styled in CSS, of course—which will display a different image based on the nature of that object.

Before we jump into any code, there is one more image worth looking at, which is shown here:

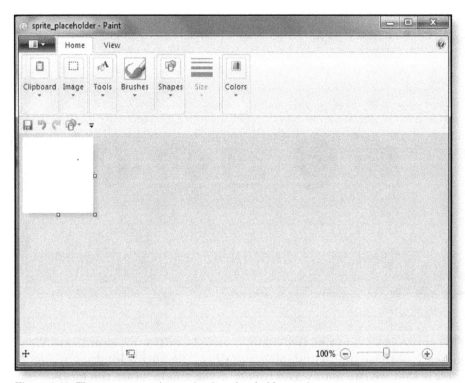

Figure 2.33: The transparent image (sprite_placeholder.png)

This is a completely transparent PNG file, measuring 110 pixels high and 110 pixels wide, which would be the width and height of each individual sprite making up our entire sprite sheet.

This 110 x 110 pixel will act as a window, showing each sprite image separately.

Take a look at our HTML code:

## CODE LISTING: SPRITE SHEET SETUP

```html
<!DOCTYPE html>
<html>
<head>
   <link rel="stylesheet" type="text/css"
href="sprites_begin.css" />
</head>

<body>
   <img id="title" src="images/sprite_
placeholder2.png" />

   <div class="chrome">Chrome:
   </div>

   <div class="ie">IE:
   </div>

   <div class="safari">Safari:
   </div>

   <div class="firefox">Firefox:
   </div>

   <div class="opera">Opera:
   </div>
</body>
</html>
```

In the browser, you will see the following:

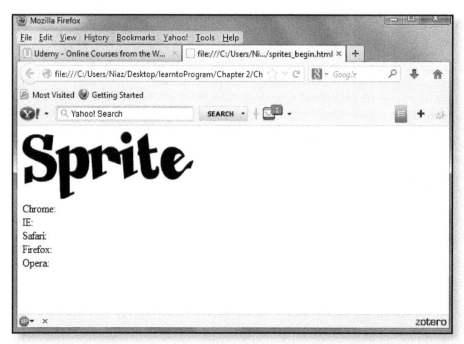

Figure 2.34: The animated text with the names of five popular browsers.

Let's analyze the code. Each of the five *div* elements has a unique class identifier, which corresponds to one of the browsers whose icons populate our sprite sheet. Our goal is to create a generic image object, which we can place within any of these *div* elements and will display the appropriate browser icon based on its parent's class. Let's go ahead and preemptively declare the *sprite* class, in the following manner:

```
<div class="chrome">Chrome:

<img class="sprite" src="images/sprite_
placeholder.png" />

</div>
```

We are doing this because we want the image object to always have the width and height of the sprite. Otherwise, it would be five times larger, and we would have to manually reduce its size, which would be a little bit confusing.

In the CSS file, we will add the sprite sheet by declaring it to be the background of our image, as shown here:

```
#title{
background: url("images/animated_sprite.
png") 0px 0px;
}

#title:hover{
background: url("images/animated_sprite.
png") -300px 0px;
}
```

Our image object could be the descendant of one of five different classes, so we will require five different CSS rules to declare which part of the sprite sheet we are going to use for each instance. So, in the CSS file, let us declare the following:

```
.chrome .sprite{
    }

.ie .sprite{

}

.safari .sprite{

}

.firefox .sprite{

}

.opera .sprite{

}
```

We should also modify the HTML file like so:

```
<!DOCTYPE html>
<html>
<head>
   <link rel="stylesheet" type="text/css"
href="sprites_end.css" />
</head>

<body>
   <img id="title" src="images/sprite_
placeholder2.png" />

   <div class="chrome">Chrome:
        <img class="sprite" src="images/
sprite_placeholder.png" />
   </div>

   <div class="ie">IE: <img class="sprite"
src="images/sprite_placeholder.png" />
   </div>

   <div class="safari">Safari: <img
class="sprite" src="images/sprite_
placeholder.png" />
   </div>

   <div class="firefox">Firefox: <img
class="sprite" src="images/sprite_
placeholder.png" />
   </div>

   <div class="opera">Opera: <img
class="sprite" src="images/sprite_
placeholder.png" />
   </div>
</body>
</html>
```

The first thing we need to do is to actually load our sprite sheet. Moreover, we need to navigate the sprite sheet to the image we desire. Let's think of our transparent image, which is in the foreground, as a window. We are only going to be able to see the piece of the sprite sheet that we've placed behind that window. By default, that would be the icon of Internet Explorer, because it's the first square of the sprite sheet that the window would cover. As we have already mentioned, our transparent image, or our window is 110 pixels wide. So, if we were to shift our sprite sheet 110 pixels to the left, our window would now be covering the icon of Firefox. So, we have to use the following in the CSS code:

```
.firefox .sprite{
background: url("images/sprite_sheet.png")
-110px 0px;
}
```

Here we have used -110 pixels because we wanted to shift the background to the left. If we wanted to shift it to the right, we would have to use a positive number. Moreover, we would need no transition to the y-axis, so we have used 0 pixels here. If our sprite sheet was styled vertically, we would of course be shifting on the y-axis and not on the x-axis at all. If the sprite sheet had multiple rows and multiple columns, we would have to shift across both the x and y-axis.

The next image in our sprite sheet is the Safari image. So, our shift for Safari is going to be 110 pixels more than we shifted for Firefox. Let's go ahead and make that -220 pixels, like this:

```
.safari .sprite{
background: url("images/sprite_sheet.png")
-220px 0px;
}
```

We can do the same thing with the images for Google Chrome, Internet Explorer and Opera, like so:

```
.chrome .sprite{
background: url("images/sprite_sheet.png")
-330px 0px;
}
```

```
.ie .sprite{
background: url("images/sprite_sheet.png")
-0px 0px;
}

.opera .sprite{
background: url("images/sprite_sheet.png")
-440px 0px;
}
```

Since we have a unique background positioning rule for each class, now we simply have to place the image object between each *div* element in the HTML code, and that alone would be sufficient to give them all unique icons. We can modify the HTML code in this way:

## CODE LISTING: SPRITE SHEET FINAL HTML

```
<!DOCTYPE html>
<html>
<head>
   <link rel="stylesheet" type="text/css"
href="sprites_end.css" />
</head>

<body>
   <img id="title" src="images/sprite_
placeholder2.png" />

   <div class="chrome">Chrome:
       <img class="sprite" src="images/
sprite_placeholder.png" />
   </div>

   <div class="ie">IE: <img class="sprite"
src="images/sprite_placeholder.png" />
   </div>
```

```
    <div class="safari">Safari: <img
class="sprite" src="images/sprite_
placeholder.png" />
    </div>

    <div class="firefox">Firefox: <img
class="sprite" src="images/sprite_
placeholder.png" />
    </div>

    <div class="opera">Opera: <img
class="sprite" src="images/sprite_
placeholder.png" />
    </div>
</body>
</html>
```

## CODE LISTING: SPRITE SHEET FINAL CSS

```
#title{
background: url("images/animated_sprite.
png") 0px 0px;
}

#title:hover{
background: url("images/animated_sprite.
png") -300px 0px;
}

.firefox .sprite{
background: url("images/sprite_sheet.png")
-110px 0px;
}
.safari .sprite{
background: url("images/sprite_sheet.png")
```

```
-220px 0px;
}

.chrome .sprite{
background: url("images/sprite_sheet.png")
-330px 0px;
}

.ie .sprite{
background: url("images/sprite_sheet.png")
-0px 0px;
}

.opera .sprite{
background: url("images/sprite_sheet.png")
-440px 0px;
}
```

If you have a look at the browser, you will see the following:

Figure 2.35: The names of five popular browsers with their corresponding icons.

We have also used a second sprite sheet here to create a page title which animates when we place our mouse over it. Here, in the HTML code, we have used the following:

```
<body>
<img id="title" src="images/sprite_
placeholder2.png" />
```

In the CSS file, we used the following code:

```
#title{
    background: url("images/animated_sprite.
png") 0px 0px;
}

#title:hover{
    background: url("images/animated_sprite.
png") -300px 0px;
}
```

At the end of this chapter, you should feel comfortable with sprite sheets, at least on a conceptual level. You are encouraged to use these as organizational tools in your web development.

## QUESTIONS FOR REVIEW

1. What are individual images in a sprite sheet called?
   a. Photos.          c. Sprites.
   b. Pixels.          d. URLs.

2. Which of the following is not an advantage of using sprite sheets?
   a. Sprite sheets look more attractive.
   b. Sprite sheets reduce the loading time of the image.
   c. It is easier to manage one single file rather than managing separate files for all the images.
   d. All of the above are advantages of using sprite sheets.

# 2.6 CREATING A DROP-DOWN MENU WITH CSS

In this section, we are going to be using both HTML and CSS together to create a brand new user interactive control, rather than simply styling an existing HTML page with CSS. Let us consider the following webpage, where you will find three separate lists:

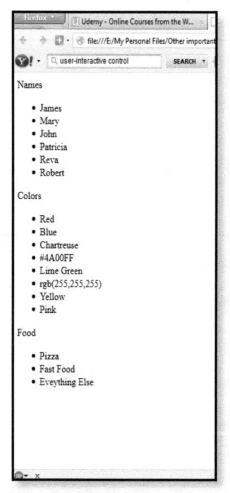

Figure 2.36: A webpage showing three different lists.

Our goal is to collapse these lists, and create a banner on the top of the page which will have 'Names', 'Colors', and 'Food' as options. Then, when the user places the mouse over one of these options, the corresponding list elements will be displayed. Generally, we call this a drop-down menu.

*CSS Development (with CSS3!)*

Let's begin by creating the structure of our drop-down menu in HTML. The initial HTML code was the following:

## CODE LISTING: DROP-DOWN MENU SETUP

```
<!DOCTYPE html>
<html>
<head>
    <link rel="stylesheet" type="text/css"
href="menu_begin.css" />
</head>

<body>

Names
<ul>
    <li>James</li>
    <li>Mary</li>
    <li>John</li>
    <li>Patricia</li>
    <li>Reva</li>
    <li>Robert</li>
</ul>

Colors
<ul>
    <li>Red</li>
    <li>Blue</li>
    <li>Chartreuse</li>
    <li>#4A00FF</li>
    <li>Lime Green</li>
    <li>rgb(255,255,255)</li>
    <li>Yellow</li>
    <li>Pink</li>
</ul>

Food
```

```
<ul>
    <li>Pizza</li>
    <li>Fast Food</li>
    <li>Eveything Else</li>
</ul>

</body>
</html>
```

Let's enclose the list in a *table* structure and enclose the *table* itself in a *div* element in the body, and assign the *div* an ID of *my_menu*, in the following manner:

```
<div id="my_menu">
</div>
```

We have done this because we are going to write a decent amount of CSS code to make our menu work as intended. What we will do is preface all of our CSS rules with the *my_menu* ID, so they never apply to anything except the menu they are intended for. Our drop-down menu has two parts: it has a banner which is always visible, and the lists which are sometimes visible. For the always visible banner, we want to use a table with only one row. Then, we want to isolate each list in its own table column, like this:

```
<body>

<div id="my_menu">
    <table>
        <tr>
            <td>
                <div class="submenu">
                    Names
                    <ul>
                        <li>James</li>
                        <li>Mary</li>
                        <li>John</li>
                        <li>Patricia</
li>
```

```
                        <li>Reva</li>
                        <li>Robert</li>
                </ul>
        </div>
    </td>
    <td>
        <div class="submenu">
            Colors
            <ul>
                <li>Red</li>
                <li>Blue</li>
                <li>Chartreuse<//
li>
                <li>#4A00FF</li>
                <li>Lime Green<//
li>

<li>rgb(255,255,255)</li>
                <li>Yellow</li>
                <li>Pink</li>
            </ul>
        </div>
    </td>
    <td>
        <div class="submenu">
            Food
            <ul>
                <li>Pizza</li>
                <li>Fast Food<//
li>
                <li>Eveything
Else</li>
            </ul>
        </div>
    </td>
        </tr>
    </table>
</div>

</body>
```

Here, we have surrounded our new list with its own *div* element, just like we did with the menu. We can't give each *div* element its unique ID because there are going to be three of them, so instead we will have them share the *sub-menu* class. Let's take a quick look at our browser:

Figure 2.37: A different way of showing the lists.

Here you can see that the horizontal and vertical structure is in place, but it certainly does not look good. To fix this, we need to work on the CSS file.

What makes our drop-down menu unique is that not all of its elements are visible all the time. So, for our first rule, let's make all the *li* elements invisible and then make them visible when you position the mouse over any of the *li* elements corresponding to either of the three top banner elements. This is the CSS code that will accomplish this.

```
#my_menu .submenu ul{
    display: none;
    }


#my_menu .submenu:hover ul{
    display: block;
}
```

Here we have used the *display* property. Since we only need to change the visual portion of the element, we would not need to change how it interacts with other elements on the page. By using the attribute *none*, we have ensured that it will neither interact with other elements, nor appear visible.

However, we don't want our submenus to be invisible all the time—we want them to be displayed when we place the mouse over them. So, we have used the *hover* property, with the attribute *block*, which will make sure that the unordered lists will be displayed when we put our mouse over the corresponding tag.

In the browser, when you position the mouse over *Colors,* you will see this:

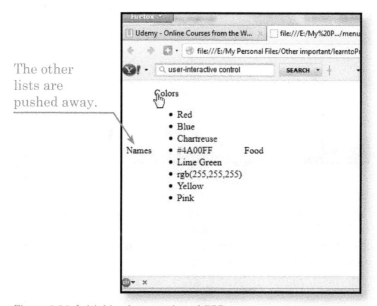

The other lists are pushed away.

Figure 2.38: Initial implementation of CSS.

However, there is a related positioning issue, where a particular unordered list pushes the other elements whenever it is being displayed. In order to avoid this, we have used the *position* property, with the attribute *fixed*, in this way:

```
#my_menu. submenu ul{
    display: none;
    position: fixed;
}
```

In the browser, you can see that an unordered list is being displayed without pushing around any of the other elements on our page. Here it is:

The other lists are *fixed*.

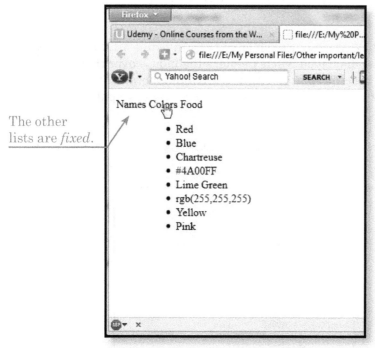

Figure 2.39: The lists are being displayed without pushing other elements.

Thus, we have created our basic functionalities regarding the drop-down menu. However, using CSS, we can try to make our menu look more attractive. So, let's do some visually appealing styling now. We'll start by giving the menu as a whole a background color, in this way:

```css
#my_menu{
    background-color: rgb(100,100,200);
}
```

This is a purple color, which will make our menu look good, as shown here:

Figure 2.40: The menu with a background color.

Another thing to notice is that the tags for our submenus are very close together. We can force them to space each other further apart by adding *padding-left* and *padding-right*, as shown here:

```
#my_menu td{
    padding-left: 15px;
    padding-right: 15px;
}
```

Take a look at how that looks in the browser:

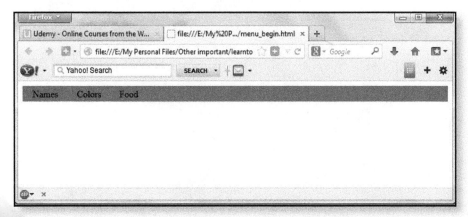

Figure 2.41: Sufficient amount of space visible between the tags.

Since we have given our menu a background color, we should give a background color to our submenus, too. Let's choose the grey color here, and modify the code in this way:

```
#my_menu .submenu ul{
    Background-color: rgb(160, 160, 160);
    display: none;
    position: fixed;
}
```

You will be happy to see the following in the browser:

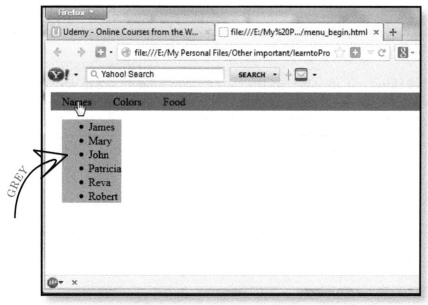

Figure 2.42: Submenu with a background color.

Here, our submenus are appearing too far down. We want them to appear just underneath their tags. If we put a border around our submenus, they will blend into the main menu as a whole much better. To do that now, we'll use the following code:

## CODE LISTING: DROP-DOWN MENU CSS

```
#my_menu. submenu ul{
    Background-color: rgb(160, 160, 160);
    border-bottom: 3px solid
rgb(100,100,200);
    border-left: 3px solid rgb(100,100,200);
    border-right: 3px solid
rgb(100,100,200);

    list-style-type: none;
    padding:10px;

    margin-top: 0px;

    display: none;
    position: fixed;
}
```

Here, in order to remove the bullets, we have used the following:

```
list-style-type: none;
```

To ensure that the edges of our submenus do not come too close to the border, we have used the *padding* option, and have chosen 10 pixels for it. Now, we need to realize that our unordered lists have a margin around them that offsets them from existing elements when they are created. If we change the width of the top margin to 0 pixels, they will be displayed right from the place where they are created, regardless of what elements are above them. We have used the following code:

```
margin-top: 0px;
```

This will remove the space between the menu and the submenu, or move the unordered list up. Viewing the browser, you will see this:

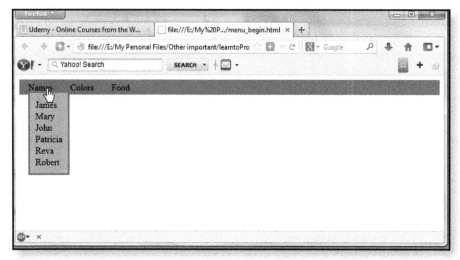

Figure 2.43: Submenu with a border around it, and no space between the main menu.

This is our fully functional drop-down menu. You can use your imagination to make these menus more visually interesting.

 QUESTIONS FOR REVIEW

1. What rule can you use to increase the space between the tags in a menu?
   a. Padding.
   b. Hovering.
   c. Underlining.
   d. Spacing.

2. Which of the following rules is used to remove bullets from the lists?
   a. list-style-type: none;
   b. list-style-type: no;
   c. list-style-type: not;
   d. list-style-type: never;

# CHAPTER 2 LAB EXERCISE

1. Start from scratch! Create a new .html webpage and associate it with a .css style sheet.

2. Add an <a> element (containing some text) to the page. Use the sliding door technique to have this element surround the text it contains with an appropriately sized graphic made from *Lab Images/right_image*.png and *Lab Images/left_image.png*.

3. Style the text within the <a> element so that it no longer looks like a link. Apply the custom font found in *Lab Images* to this text.

4. Modify the <a> element so that its text is only partially visible unless it is hovered over. The visible container should look complete in both display states.

5. Create a 2x2 table on your page. Place a copy of your <a> element in each of the table's four cells. Apply borders to the table's cells – watch them react to changes in their content area when you hover over the <a> elements.

6. Set *Lab Images/background.png* to be the background image of the webpage. Set each instance of the background to a fixed width and height of 300x300 pixels.

7. Allow the background to repeat along the X and Y axes.

The images are given here:

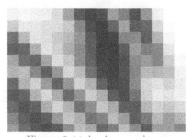

Figure 2.44: background.png

Figure 2.45: left_image.png

Figure 2.46: right_image.png

# Chapter 2 Summary

In this chapter we learned how to style the texts on a page in a variety of ways using CSS. We need to use different types of fonts on our webpage, and this chapter taught us how to do that. We also discussed changing the background color of a table and the various techniques available for styling ordered and unordered lists on a webpage.

We gained some valuable knowledge regarding the sliding door technique and its use for creating nicely shaped buttons for our webpage. Moreover, as the background is a big contributing factor to making a webpage really stylish, we have learned how to beautify a webpage by modifying the background in the way that we prefer.

We have also understood what a sprite sheet is and how to use a sprite sheet to display a group of images at a time. Finally, we have realized how to create a drop-down menu for the webpage and learned how to do useful things with it using CSS.

In the next chapter, we will learn what a box model is, and also the effects of changing the different attributes that contribute to the box model.

# CHAPTER 3

# THE BOX MODEL

## CHAPTER OBJECTIVES:

- You will understand the effects of changing the different style properties that contribute to the box model and the look and feel of the components of the box model.
- You will learn how to effectively deal with resizing images and image and text content overflow.
- You will know the options available to you when styling borders and outlines.
- You will learn how to work with margins and padding and become aware of problems you may run into while working with various settings of these properties.

## 3.1 INTRODUCTION TO THE BOX MODEL

As far as CSS is concerned, every HTML element exists within a box surrounded by different areas, as shown below. The HTML element (text, image, etc.) which has its own *width* and *height* is surrounded by a *padding* area, and then a *border* area and finally a *margin* area. Each of these box's areas has properties which you can set and modify. The HTML element (text, image, etc.) which is also called the *content*, the *padding*, the *border*, and the *margin* make up the *CSS Box Model*. On a webpage, all HTML elements exist within a *Box Model* which is shown graphically below.

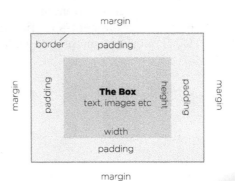

Let's consider the following webpage:

Figure 3.1: A webpage with an image, or an HTML element.

In this page, the image is an HTML element, which means that it exists in a box model. The manner in which it displays and positions both in regards to the page as a whole and the elements surrounding it, in this case the text, is affected by four of its box model areas: the content layer, the padding, the border, and the margin. Additionally, the way it looks to us is affected by a sixth component: the outline layer.

We are going to be modifying these areas, one by one, starting with the content, the innermost area. The content area, or the innermost rectangle of the box model, is where all of our element-specific information goes. In order to work with our HTML element, or the image, let's consider the following HTML code:

## CODE LISTING: INTRO TO THE BOX MODEL HTML

```
<!DOCTYPE html>
<html>
<head>
   <link rel="stylesheet" type="text/css"
href="box_model_begin.css" />
</head>

<body>
        Lorem ipsum dolor sit amet,
consectetur adipisicing elit, sed do
eiusmod tempor incididunt ut labore et
dolore magna aliqua. Ut enim ad minim
veniam, quis nostrud exercitation ullamco
laboris nisi ut aliquip ex ea commodo ……..

        <img src="image.jpg"
class="image"/>

        Lorem ipsum dolor sit amet,
consectetur adipisicing elit, sed do
eiusmod tempor incididunt ut labore et
dolore magna aliqua. Ut enim ad minim
veniam, quis nostrud exercitation ullamco
laboris nisi ut aliquip ex ea commodo
consequat. Duis aute ……………………………

in reprehenderit in voluptate velit esse
cillum dolore eu fugiat nulla pariatur.
Excepteur sint occaecat cupidatat non
proident, sunt in culpa qui officia deserunt
mollit anim id est laborum.

</body>
</html>
```

Take a look at the corresponding CSS code:

CODE LISTING: INTRO TO THE BOX MODEL CSS

```css
    .image{
    background-color: green;
    float:left;

    width: inherit;
    height: inherit;

    padding: 0 0 0 0;
    border: none;
    margin: 0 0 0 0;
    outline: none;
}
```

Since we are working with a rectangular image, the size of the image that we see in our web browser is going to fit the size of the content area that we have declared. Right now, the content area is set to encompass the entire image in its default width and height. We can modify the element's content area by changing its *width* and *height* property values. It's really important to understand that when we change an HTML element's *width* and *height*, we are only modifying the size of its content area. For example, let's modify the CSS code in this way:

```css
width: 200px;
height: 200px;
```

Here we assume that an element whose width and height are both 200 pixels will never affect the position, vertically and horizontally, of other elements that are 100 pixels from the center of the former. This isn't the case always, however, because 200 pixels x 200 pixels is only the width and height of the content area in the element's box model. Its padding, border, and margin can all have their own physical space that fall outside the content area. For now, let's modify the size of our image to be a little smaller by just setting its width to 200 pixels and removing the following part of the code:

```
height: 200px;
```

If we see the webpage, we will be able to easily find out that the image is shrunk to the new size, in the following manner:

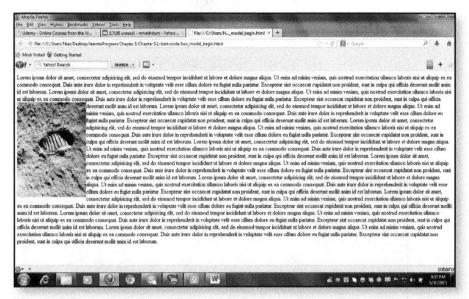

Figure 3.2: The image is shrunk in the webpage.

Here, since we did not define the height explicitly, the *aspect ratio* of the image, that is, the ratio of its *width* and *height* as an image file, remains at its default setting.

Now, let's talk about padding. We use padding to increase the space an object takes up without actually increasing the size of the object's content area. So, if we were to add 5 pixels of padding to all sides of our object then we would displace more text without making the actual image any larger.

```
padding: 5px 5px 5px 5px;
```

You may also have noticed that our object has a background color, declared in this way:

```
background-color: green;
```

However, we do not see any background color yet, because the image takes up the object's entire area thus covering the background. But now, with padding, we get 5 pixels of the object's background color outside of our original image, as shown here:

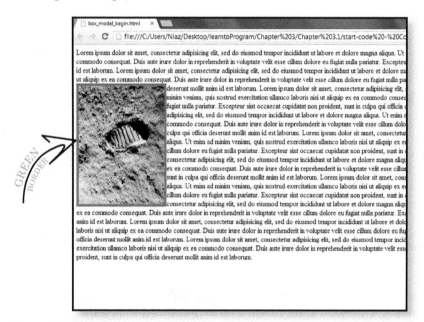

Figure 3.3: The image with a background color in the outside area.

Consider the border of our image object. The border is going to affect both the positioning and the display of our object as a whole. This means that the border will become visible and will add space to the display area of the image without affecting the size of the image.

We generally style a border by giving it three property values: a width (5px), a style (dashed) and a color (black):

```
border: 5px dashed black;
```

Take a look at your web browser:

Figure 3.4: The image with a styled border.

If you look between the border's dashes, you can see our green background color. Note also that padding does not hide the background.

Now let's explore the margin's property values. Since margins are not affected by our object's border, we should expect it to be completely transparent, otherwise it's just like padding that appears outside of the border of the element rather than inside the border and outside of the content area. Because margins are transparent, we generally use it to put space between an object and the other objects surrounding it. Let's go ahead and add a 15 pixel margin to each side of the object, in the following manner:

```
margin: 15px 15px 15px 15px;
```

In the web browser, you will find this:

Figure 3.5: The image with a margin around it. You can see the space in its surrounding area, separating it from the text.

The last layer of the box model is the outline. While the margin is simply a positional element and does not have any display properties, the outline is purely a display element and has no positioning properties. No matter how ridiculous an outline we create, it won't affect the positioning of anything on our page. To illustrate this, let's add a sizeable outline to our element. We declare outlines just like we do for the borders. Here, we'll declare the following:

```
outline: 30px solid red;
```

Here we have defined the outline to be 30 pixels because we want it to be wider than our margin. Let's also have a solid red line around our image. In the browser, you will see the following:

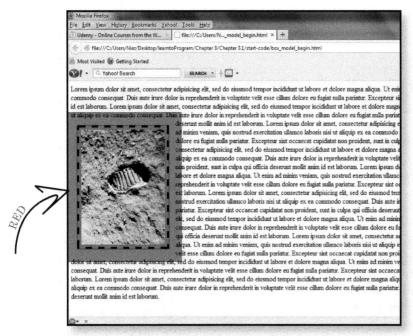

Figure 3.6: The image with a beautiful outline.

Here, the outline travels from our border, through our margin, and even through some of the text surrounding the object. The outline is able to do that because it's a purely visual element. It has no positioning information, so it does not displace the text surrounding the image. If we made our margin 30 pixels, then it would have displaced the text in the area colored red by our outline.

So, these are all the pieces of the box model: content, surrounded by padding, which is surrounded by the border, which is eventually surrounded both by the margin and the outline. Exploring the box model is a new phase in our development as CSS developers. Rather than focusing on a single object, we look at our webpage as a whole and style how the elements interact with each other.

QUESTIONS FOR REVIEW

1. How many layers are there in a box model?
   a. One.
   b. Three.
   c. Five.
   d. Seven.

2. Which of the following is not a layer in the box model?
   a. Margin Layer.
   b. Padding Layer.
   c. Outline Layer.
   d. Display Layer.

*CSS Development (with CSS3!)*

# 3.2 THE CONTENT AREA

In this section, we are going to learn to two things. First, we will explore how HTML images and HTML text elements are handled when we resize their content areas, specifically when we make their content areas too small for the elements to display comfortably at their default size. The second thing we will do is explore the CSS 'overflow' property which allows us to explicitly define how an element handles the content area which is too small for it. The webpage that we will style contains only two elements: an image and a paragraph which are shown here:

Figure 3.7: A webpage with an image and a paragraph element.

Let's look at the corresponding HTML code:

## CODE LISTING: CONTENT AREA EXAMPLE HTML

```
<!DOCTYPE html>
<html>
<head>
    <link rel="stylesheet" type="text/css"
href="content_begin.css" />
</head>
```

```
<body>
        <div id="scroll_box">
            <img src="image.jpg"
id="image"/>
        </div>
        <br>
        <br>
        <br>
        <p id="text">
            Lorem ipsum dolor sit amet,
consectetur adipisicing elit, sed do
eiusmod tempor incididunt ut labore et
dolore magna aliqua. Ut enim ad minim
veniam, quis nostrud exercitation ullamco
laboris nisi ut aliquip ex ea commodo
consequat. Duis aute irure dolor in
reprehenderit in voluptate velit esse
cillum dolore eu fugiat nulla pariatur.
Excepteur sint occaecat cupidatat non
proident, sunt in culpa qui officia deserunt
mollit anim id est laborum.
        </p>
</body>
</html>
```

And also the CSS code:

## CODE LISTING: CONTENT AREA EXAMPLE CSS

```
#scroll_box{
}

#image{
    padding: 0 0 0 0;
    border:none;
    margin: 0 0 0 0;
    outline: 2px dashed red;
```

```
    }

#text{
    padding: 0 0 0 0;
    border:none;
    margin: 0 0 0 0;
    outline: 2px dashed red;
}
```

You can see that we have assigned id selectors to our image and text elements. We also did some preliminary styling, where we removed the padding, border and margin from both image and paragraph elements but we applied a dotted red outline. With no padding, border, or margin, the outline will surround the content area of both elements.

To begin our exploration, let's set the width for our image element to 200px (200 pixels). Now, instead of setting the width of our text element in pixels we will use a percentage value of 20%. That is 20% of the text element's containing element, which is the body of the page, so the width of the text element should be 20% of the page's width. Modify the code in the following manner:

```
#scroll_box{
}

#image{
    padding: 0 0 0 0;
    border:none;
    margin: 0 0 0 0;
    outline: 2px dashed red;

    width: 200px;
}

#text{
    padding: 0 0 0 0;
    border:none;
    margin: 0 0 0 0;
    outline: 2px dashed red;
```

```
    width: 20%;
}
```

If we have a look at the webpage, we will find the following:

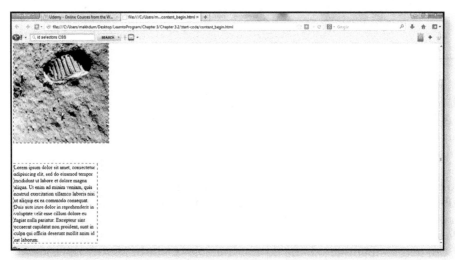

Figure 3.7: A webpage with an image and a paragraph element, with modified width.

Here you can see that both elements have shrunk to accommodate the changes in the width. What we want to show is how the height of these elements change as a result. In the previous picture, you can see that the height of our image element has actually decreased. This is because image elements, by default, try to maintain their aspect ratio when only either the width or height is changed. Because it's much easier for CSS elements to push page contents vertically than horizontally, this is much more reliable when we change the width of our image, than when we change the height.

On the other hand, the height of our text box has grown so that all the text can fit perfectly in the text box using new lines. Now, let's see what happens if we separately set the height of the elements. Let's set the height of our image as 100 pixels:

```
#image{

height: 100px;
}
```

We could set the height of our text element in percentages, but because webpages can freely resize themselves vertically, our very simple page here would just resize itself until the high percentage of our text element was a reasonable height for our text to display. So we are going to switch our height and width to pixels, in the following manner:

```
#text{
    width: 200px;
    height: 200px;
}
```

If we look at our browser, we will see the following:

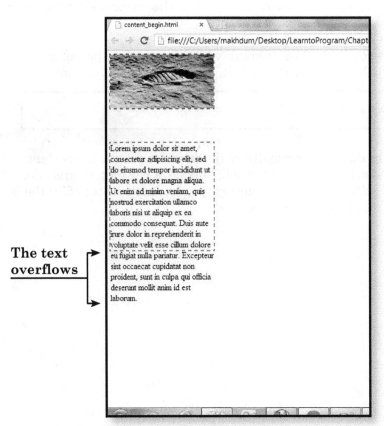

The text overflows

Figure 3.8: The image and text elements are shrunken as their heights are explicitly defined.

Here you can see that our image has compressed itself to fit the width of 200 pixels and the height of 100 pixels. However, the text element did not resize itself—instead, it simply spilled or overflowed its contents outside its content area. This is the default behavior of images and text. When an image is placed in a content area that it cannot comfortably resize according to its aspect ratio, it will resize across the X and Y axis independently. When we place text in a content area which cannot accommodate all its text, it will spill its contents vertically. We could even cause the text to spill horizontally if we make the content area's display width too narrow.

What we are going to do now is explore the CSS **overflow** property. With this property, we can change the way that our image and text elements display their contents as the width and height of their display areas decreases. Using this property, we can ensure that the text does not display outside the borders of its content box, and that the image displays at its full size, regardless of the size of its content box.

overflow

There are five possible values or options for this **overflow** property: scroll, auto, visible, hidden, and inherit. This is the default option:

```
overflow: visible;
```

The text will be displayed normally, with some of it outside the content box. Now, we don't want the text to spill outside of our content area. So, if we use the *hidden* option, then our text would simply be cut off at the dashed border that we can see here:

Figure 3.9: The text is cut off at the border.

However, we want to make sure that our entire text is displayed perfectly. So, we can use either the *scroll*, or the *auto* option. If we choose the *scroll* option, we would see vertical and horizontal scrollbars that would let us navigate our text block and see all of it in the small window of its content area. However, our text will only be cut off vertically, because of the way the *overflow* is handled, so we don't need the horizontal scrollbar. Hence, we should use the *auto* option here. *Auto* will apply scrollbars only where they would be relevant. If we were to use this option here, we would see this in the browser:

Figure 3.10: The text box with a vertical scrollbar.

Here, the vertical scrollbar will allow us to scroll the content area like its own window and view the text in its entirety. Now, we want our image to overflow in the same manner as our text. We use the following code:

```
#image{

overflow: visible;

}
```

We will see that no change occurs in the webpage, because our image is perfectly happy to simply resize its width and height to the width and height of the small content area we gave it. It's not actually overflowing its content box at all. We can fix this issue by modifying the entire CSS code like this:

```
#scroll_box{
    width: 200px;
    height: 100px;
    overflow: visible;

    padding: 0 0 0 0;
    border:none;
    margin: 0 0 0 0;
    outline: 2px dashed red;
}

#image{
}

#text{
    padding: 0 0 0 0;
    border:none;
    margin: 0 0 0 0;
    outline: 2px dashed red;

    width: 200px;
    height: 200px;
    overflow: auto;
}
```

Viewing it in the web browser, we will see this:

Figure 3.11: The image is displayed in its entirety.

You can see the entire image, even though the content area of that containing box is too small to display the image in its entirety. We also notice that the image has overlapped the text here. This is because the overflowed image is not a content box, it's just an HTML element, so it doesn't have the positioning information of the content box that would tell the text element to move down to stay away from the image area.

The last thing we are going to see is what happens if we use the following in the CSS code:

```
#scroll_box{

    overflow: hidden;
}
```

We see that rather than having an image that resizes, we see a part of the image based on the size of our content box, as shown here:

Figure 3.12: Only a part of the image is shown.

By now, you should be fairly comfortable with how CSS handles the content area of images and texts and also with the **overflow** property.

## QUESTIONS FOR REVIEW

1. Which property allows us to explicitly define how an element handles the content area which is too small for it?
   a. Overflow.           c. Explore.
   b. Inline.             d. Display.

2. Which of the following is not a possible value for the *overflow* property?
   a. Scroll.             c. Visible.
   b. Auto.               d. Invisible.

# 3.3 BORDER AND OUTLINE STYLING

In this chapter we discuss styling borders and outlines. Many CSS2 style properties for borders and outlines have been retained in CSS3, but we will look at style properties unique to CSS3.

The page we are going to modify contains only a single image, which we will style through a CSS class in the following manner:

```
#image{
    padding:5px;
}
```

Let's see the corresponding HTML code:

```
<!DOCTYPE html>
<html>
<head>
    <link rel="stylesheet" type="text/css"
href="borders_outlines_begin.css" />
</head>

<body>
    <img src="image.jpg" id="image"/>
</body>
</html>
```

First, let's begin by adding a border to this image. We want to make sure that our borders and outlines have *border-style* and *outline-style* properties explicitly declared. There are a lot of options available for these properties, and fortunately these options are also available in CSS2. These options are given here as comments in the CSS code:

```
/*border-style and outline-style options:
solid
    dotted
```

```
    dashed
    double

    grove
    ridge
    inset
    outset

hidden
*/
```

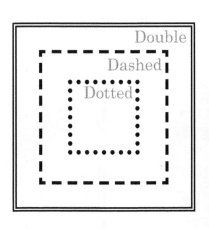
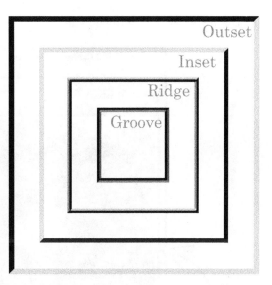

The above options are divided into three groups. The bottom or last group has only one option. If you set your *border-style* to *hidden*, the border won't be displayed at all:

```
#image{
    padding: 5px;
    border-style: hidden;
}
```

There is a major difference between the first two groups. The styling options of the second group, *grove, ridge, inset* and *outset*, will also be changing parts of your border's color to give it a three-dimensional look.

On the other hand, the options in the first group, *solid, dotted, dashed,* and *double,* will be either rendering pixels of your border's pure color or transparency. Let's choose the *inset* option here like this:

```
border-style: inset;
```

The other two properties we want to make sure get declared here are *color* and *width,* which we choose in the following way:

```
border-color: red;
border-width: 5px;
```

In the browser, you will see this:

Figure 3.13: The image with a styled border.

Here you can see that the top and left-hand sides of the border are a darker color than the right and bottom sides. This is the result of the *inset* property value of the *border-style* property through which we are attempting to give our border a three-dimensional look.

Before we move on to the CSS3 part, let's quickly cover the short way to style borders and outlines. Rather than using the options separately, we can declare them one at a time on a single line, like this:

```
#image{
    padding: 5px;
    border: 5px inset red;
}
```

Just for borders, we can also style individual sides separately:

```
#image{
    padding: 5px;
    border: 5px inset red;
    border-color: red green blue purple;
}
```

In the browser, you will see the following:

Figure 3.14: The image with four different colors in the border.

CSS3 offers a cool option when styling borders. We can use the **border-radius** property to create borders with rounded corners which was difficult to achieve in CSS2. With the **border-radius** property, we can create rounded borders using only CSS. Being a CSS3 feature, we need to be conscious about which browsers support the **border-radius** property in its entirety. Currently, all major web browsers support **border-radius**. Let's analyze the corresponding CSS code:

```
#image{
    padding: 5px;
    border: 5px inset red;
    border-color: red green blue purple;
    border-radius: 15px;
    -moz-border-radius: 15px;

}
```

Even though the current version of Mozilla Firefox supports the **border-radius** property, here we have used the *-moz-border-radius* property to make sure that older versions of Firefox will support it. In the browser, you will see this:

Figure 3.15: The border with rounded corners.

We can also style an individual corner of our border. If we wanted a rounded border only in the top left corner, we would have written this:

```
border-top-left-radius: 15px;
```

Next we are going to discuss another CSS3 property, **border-image**. Using **border-image**, we can take an image file and turn it into a border that we can place around any element. So, here is our image:

Figure 3.16: image_border.png

It's important that this image already resembles a border, because what we are going to do is divide this image into nine parts. Four of these parts are going to be the four corners of the border, and another four are going to be the areas between the corners. These areas will either repeat or stretch to fill whatever space we give them. Our last part is the internal section of the border image, where the content area, or the area within the border, will go. The important thing for us to know about the image right now is that the distance from any side to our content area is 26 pixels.

Let's modify the code in this way:

```
#image{
padding:5px;
border: 1px inset red;
border-image: url("image_border.png") 26 26
repeat;
-moz-border-image: url("image_border.png")
26 26 repeat;
-webkit-border-image: url("image_border.
png") 26 26 repeat;
-o-border-image: url("image_border.png") 26
26 repeat;
}
```

Here, we used the **border-image** property, which is specific to CSS3. Internet Explorer does not support it. However, all of the other major browsers support it to some degree, hence we have used the browser particular syntax to use this property here. Make sure that the image that we are using here is put in the same folder where our CSS file is located. And once we've told the **border-image** property where to find the image, we need to instruct it how to cut off our image to create the nine sections we have just talked about. It's going to cut the image in four sides: top, bottom, right and left, and in 26 pixels. In the code, we are doing it in the following manner:

```
border-image: url("image_border.png") 26 26
repeat;
```

We have also declared the top and bottom distances as one value (26) and the right and left distances also as one value (26). Also note that if you use "26px" in the code, it will not work. This is something that is peculiar to CSS3 and this has something to do with the fact that CSS3 is designed to support vector images as well as standard images which use pixels. We can also declare these distances in terms of percentages of the entire image's width or height.

The last thing we did here is to instruct the border image how we want the space between corners to display itself. We could choose *repeat* or *stretch*. Here we have chosen the *repeat* option, because we expect the area between the corners of our image to repeat itself to fill the entire area.

Viewing it in the browser, you will see this:

You can see that the border being displayed here is very small. This is because we set only 5 pixels as the width of the border. If you change it to 20 pixels, you will see this:

Figure 3.17: The image is displayed in the border.

Figure 3.18: The width of the border has been increased.

In this chapter, you should have gained a clear understanding of different ways to style borders. You can also style outlines, which are styled just like borders in CSS.

## QUESTIONS FOR REVIEW

1. Which of the following options can we use to ensure that the border won't be displayed at all?
   a. inline.
   b. hidden.
   c. vanished.
   d. ridge.

2. Which of the following options is used to give our border a three-dimensional look?
   a. inset.
   b. dotted.
   c. double.
   d. solid.

# 3.4 WORKING WITH MARGINS AND PADDING

In this chapter we discuss additional features of margins and padding style properties. We will go over some techniques, take a look at a few features, and learn when to use one over the other.

The page that we are going to be working with currently contains five images, as shown here:

Figure 3.19: The webpage with five similar images.

Although you may only see four images, the box at the bottom is actually two images placed next to each other. The intention when creating this page was for the middle pair of images to be styled just like the box on the bottom, but as you can see, there is a space between the middle pair of images.

If we take a look at our CSS code, we will see that there is only a single class rule selector. It explicitly declares that anything with this class will have no padding, no margin, and no border, as shown here:

```
.small-box{
    padding: 0 0 0 0;
    margin: 0 0 0 0;
    border: none;
}
```

Let's take a look at the corresponding HTML code:

## CODE LISTING: MARGINS & PADDING HTML

```
<!DOCTYPE html>
<html>
<head>
    <link rel="stylesheet" type="text/css"
href="margin_padding_begin.css" />
</head>

<body>
    <img id="split-image" src="images/left_
half.png"/>

    <br><br><br><br>

    <img id="top-p" class="small-box"
src="images/left_half.png"/>
    <img id="bottom-p" class="small-box"
src="images/right_half.png"/>

    <br><br><br><br>

    <img id="top-m" class="small-
box" src="images/left_half.png"/><img
id="bottom-m" class="small-box"
src="images/right_half.png"/>
</body>
</html>
```

The reason that we see a space between the middle pair of images is that there is a new line between the HTML of the first and second image. The bottom pair of images does not have a new line between the HTML of the two images. However, if we modify the code for the middle pair of images and remove the new line, then we will see this:

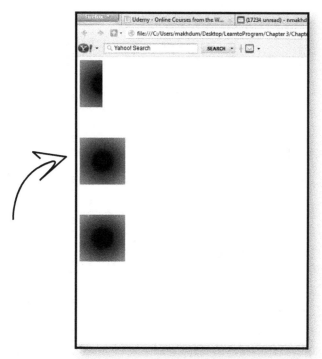

Figure 3.20: The middle pair of images are merged, with no space between them.

Although this is not an issue regarding margin or padding, we discuss it here because anyone can make a mistake in this case which can be easily overlooked. Now, let's style the top part of our page so that it looks like the middle and bottom parts. We could of course just add another image next to this one by simply adding a line in the HTML code, but let's see if we can do it just in CSS. You can add the following CSS code:

```
#split-image{
    background-image: url('images/right_
half.png');
    background-position: right top;
    padding-right: 50px;
}
```

Here we use the *sliding door technique* that has already been discussed in the previous chapter, and have loaded the second image file as the background. Applying this code will insert the second image to the right of the first image, as shown here:

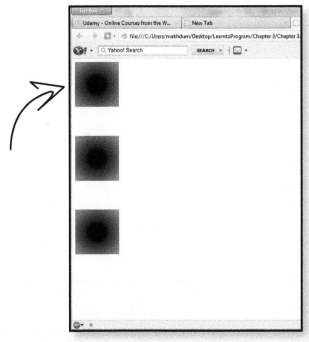

Figure 3.21: The second image is added to the right of the first image in the top part.

Here you can see that these elements are not flush with the sides of our page, because there is a margin around the body of the page. We can change that by accessing the page's body and setting its margin to zero, like this:

```
body{
    margin: 0 0 0 0;
}
```

Now our elements will display perfectly flush, as shown here:

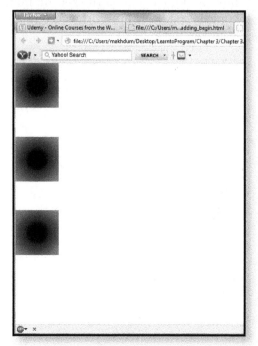

Figure 3.22: Elements are perfectly flush.

Let's explore one more instance which sometimes seems confusing. Here, we modify the CSS code in this way:

```
#split-image{
    background-image: url('images/right_
half.png');
    background-position: right top;
    padding-right: 50px;
}

#left-p
{
    padding-bottom: 10px;
}
    #right-p
    {
        padding-top: 10px;
    }
```

*CSS Development (with CSS3!)*

```
#left-m
{
    margin-bottom: 10px;
}
    #right-m
    {
        margin-top:10px;
    }

.small-box{
    display: block;
    padding: 0 0 0 0;
    margin: 0 0 0 0;
    border: none;
}

body{
    margin: 0 0 0 0;
}
```

In the browser, you will see this:

Figure 3.23: The images are separated by margins and padding.

Let's analyze the code. Here, we have changed the display of the second and third collections to be *block*, rather than *inline*. This has caused them to display one on top of another rather than next to each other.

We have also set up id selectors for all of these elements, so there are four id selectors in total. We have separated the first two elements using padding, and the last two elements using margins, as shown here:

## CODE LISTING: MARGINS & PADDING CSS

```css
#left-p
{
    padding-bottom: 10px;
}

    #right-p
    {
            padding-top: 10px;
    }

#left-m
{
     margin-bottom: 10px;
}

    #right-m
    {
            margin-top:10px;
    }
```

In the browser, you can see that the images are separated by padding and margins, but even though we have declared the same pixel size of our padding and margins, the elements separated by margins are separated by less distance than the elements separated by padding. Specifically, they are separated by half of the distance. This is the CSS feature known as margin-collapse. We generally see it in the horizontal margins, which determine how far above or below the images are from each other. CSS generally determines when a margin-collapse is appropriate in an efficient way. It's there so that your webpages compress to the smallest vertical size that is reasonable for maximum viewer experience. Margin-collapse, for example, won't occur on elements whose *overflow* property is set to anything besides *visible*, and it won't occur on elements that are displayed as *in-line block*.

It's important to remember that CSS has very specific purposes for padding and margins. Changing padding allows us to modify the element-specific area of our HTML. We can use padding to increase or decrease the size of an element's background area, for example, things that display and appear and also function like part of the element. Whereas margins are intended to be used to describe how an element displays and places on a page in terms of the other elements on the page and their margins.

In this chapter we have learned some advanced techniques regarding margins and padding, which can be really useful while designing our webpages.

QUESTIONS FOR REVIEW

1. Which rule defines that the elements separated by margins are separated by less distance than the elements separated by padding?
   a. margin-collapse
   b. margin-distance
   c. margin-add
   d. padding-collapse

# CHAPTER 3 LAB EXERCISE

1. Assign a new CSS style sheet to the LabBegin.html page (also, make sure the image path is correct). Create id selection rules targeting the <div> and <img> elements on the page.

2. Modify the page's <div> element to be the same width and height as the <img>. The image file used is 400x300 pixels. While you're at it, assign the <div> element a non-white background color. The image is given here:

Figure 3.24: The image to be used in the exercise.

3. Add an "overflow:" line to the <div>'s CSS rule so that users may use a scrollbar to view any text outside the 400x300 pixel area.

4. Use negative margin to allow the page's image to display over the <div> and its contents.

5. Modify the <img> element, through its id selector, so that it disappears (or at least flickers) when the page viewer mouses over it (the text beneath should be visible when this happens). Hint: try "visibility: hidden;"

6. Make the system more robust (no flickering image on mouse movement) by wrapping the existing <div> and <img> tags with a new <div>. Now, apply the *hidden* state to your image when the surrounding <div> is hovered over.

7. Add padding to the <div> so that the scrollbar (and only the scrollbar) is no longer covered by the lock image.

8. Add 5 pixels of black around the edge of your widget. This can be accomplished with either a border or an outline. Find an instance where each rule works.

9. Can you move the object we've created so that it displays in the center of the page?

> (**Hint:** Use position:absolute;, left:%, right:%, and negative margins.)

# CHAPTER 3 SUMMARY

In this chapter we learned the basic concepts regarding the box model, and the effects of changing the different style properties that contribute to the box model. We now have a clear idea regarding the five different areas of a box model: content, padding, border, margin, and outline.

We explored how HTML images and HTML text elements behave when we resize their content areas, specifically when we make their content areas too small for the elements to display comfortably at their default sizes. We dealt with the CSS 'overflow' property which allows us to define how an element handles the content area which is too small for it.

We also gained a clear understanding of styling borders and outlines in different ways and learned some advanced techniques regarding margins and padding.

In the next chapter, we will learn how CSS is used to transform elements, like how to rotate, skew or scale elements using CSS. You will also learn how to effectively use animations using CSS.

# CHAPTER 4

# ANIMATIONS WITH CSS3

## CHAPTER OBJECTIVES:

- You will understand how to use the CSS3 transform property.
- You will learn how to rotate, scale, and skew an element along two and three dimensions.
- You will understand the use of transitions and their multiple aspects.
- You will learn how to use CSS3 animation.

## 4.1 CSS3 TRANSFORMS

In this chapter we will be taking a look at an in-development CSS3 feature: the **transform** property.

 This property allows us to rotate, scale, skew, and even reposition the visual portions of our element, while essentially keeping their margins where they used to be so that the rest of our page is unaffected.

Eventually, *transform* will allow us to do all these things in three-dimentional space, which is a new concept for web development. However, this is currently supported by only a couple of web browsers, and it is supported in a very rudimentary sense. In this chapter, we will be going over how the basics of 3D *transform* work. By learning the basics, you will be prepared when all the web browsers support 3D *transform* to a significant degree.

The page that we are going to modify in this chapter contains two identical image elements right next to each other, as shown here:

Figure 4.1: The webpage showing two identical images.

In the corresponding HTML file, we have the following code:

## CODE LISTING: TRANSFORMS HTML

```html
<!DOCTYPE html>
<html>
<head>
    <link rel="stylesheet" type="text/css"
href="transforms_begin.css" />
</head>

<body>
     <img src="image.jpg" class="image"
id="left"/><img src="image.jpg"
class="image" id="right"/>
</body>
</html>
```

Let's also take a look at the CSS code:

## CODE LISTING: TRANSFORMS CSS

```
body{
}

.image{
   float: left;

   background-color: green;
   padding: 10px 10px 10px 10px;
   border: 1px dashed black;
   margin: 10px 10px 10px 10px;
   outline: 10px solid red;
}

#left{
}
   #left:hover{
   }

#right{
}
   #right:hover{
   }
```

Here you can see that we have created separate ID selectors for these two images. We have also given them visible borders, outlines, and padding as well as set a green background color. By doing this, we ensure that through the *transform* property, we will modify not only the content area of the image elements but also their padding, borders, and outlines.

Before we jump into any code, let's analyze what it means to us as developers that we are working with an in-development CSS feature. *Transform* is listed in W3C as a working draft. This means that the specifications of *transform* that the W3C has come up with are probably just going to stay the way they are, but W3C reserves the right to change that. This is the reason that not all major browsers have fully supported *transform* yet. Specifically, three-dimensional *transform* is supported by only two browsers: Google Chrome and Safari. On the flip side, this

As of 2013, 3-D *transform* is supported only by Google Chrome and Safari Browsers

means that a couple of the features that we need to work around and will be discussing in this chapter may not be present in the final CSS3 implementations of all the browsers.

To begin with, let's explore 2D transforms. These are transforms that operate solely on the X- and Y-axis that traditional web development has been confined to. All major web browsers currently support 2D transforms.

We can use four different types of transforms to change our object's display. These are: **translate**, which repositions an object; **rotate**, which rotates an object; **scale**, which will stretch an object in one of the available directions; and finally **skew**, which we will explore last. However, we access all of these options through a single style property, which is **transform.** It is a CSS3 feature, and no major web browsers currently use the *transform* style, they all use alternative naming. So, we need to write

**2D Transforms:**
→ **translate**
→ **rotate**
→ **scale**
→ **skew**

identical rules for all of our *transform* styles. In the CSS code, we use it in the following manner:

```
#left{
}
    #left:hover{
        -moz-transform:
        -webkit-transform:
        -ms-transform:
        -o-transform:
    }
```

Here, we will be viewing our webpage in Google Chrome, so we will only use the *–webkit-* rule here. Let's make our first goal to move our left image to the right by 90 pixels when we hover over it. In order to do this, we'll use the following code:

```
#left:hover{
        -webkit-transform: translate(90px);
    }
```

The *translate* will occur to the right, because that's the default *translate* direction. All of our *transform* rules also have slightly different wordings. For example, if we wanted to *translate* our image upwards, we would use the following:

**translate**

```
#left:hover{
        -webkit-transform:
translateY(90px);
    }
```

Here, we should explicitly say *translateX,* so that there is no confusion, as we want to move it to the right. The positive X is used when we want to move the element to the right, and the positive Y is used when we want to move it upwards. In the browser, you will see this:

Figure 4.2: The left image is moved to the right by 90 pixels.

As you can see here, the image to the right did not react in any way.

Essentially, we have moved all of the left-hand side image except for the margin which we have left just the way it is, so that the positioning of the other elements on our page has not been changed.

We can also stretch or compress the elements on our page using the **scale** property of the *transform* style. Just like the *translate* property, *scale* is equivalent to *scaleX*, as we want to scale across the X axis. We can also use *scaleY* here, when needed. Rather than giving pixels, we give a fraction amount to scale an element.

So, if we use *scale* in this way:

**scale**

```
#left{
-webkit-transform: scaleX(2.0);
    }
```

Then we will see that the left-hand image element will be twice the size of the original, as shown here:

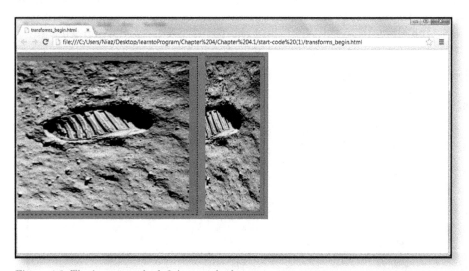

Figure 4.3: The image on the left is stretched.

If we want to reduce the size of the image to half of its current size across the Y axis, we should modify the code in this way:

```
#left{
-webkit-transform: scaleY(0.5);
}
```

In the browser, you will see this:

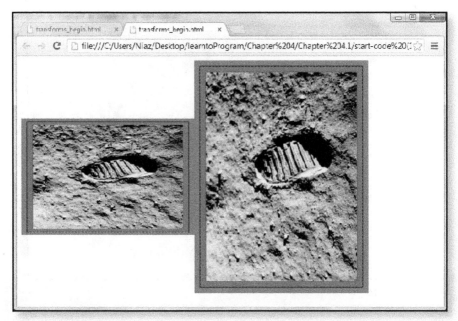

Figure 4.4: The image on the left is now half of its previous size.

Here you need to keep in mind that the *hover* rule is more specific than the general *id selection* rule, so when we put our mouse over the image element, the *translate* rule works instead of the *scale* rule. This of course does not mean that we can't have both the *translate* and *scale* rule exist in synchrony. We just need to declare them both on the same line, in the following way:

```
#left:hover{
    -webkit-transform: scaleY(0.5)
translateX(90px);
}
```

This is what you will see in the browser:

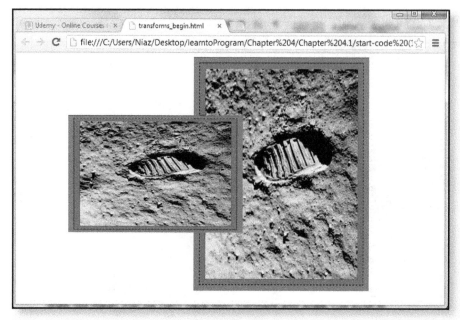

Figure 4.4: Here, both the scale and translate property are displayed at the same time.

Here you can see that the left image still moves to the right while maintaining the 50% scaling.

Transforms also allow us to change how the elements on our page look by skewing them. Let's say that all of the elements on our page are contained in a box, which they are in reality. This box, by default, contains two horizontal and two vertical sides which intersect at right angles, that is, 90 degrees. When we change an object's skew, we are actually changing the angles of intersection. So, a skew of 0 degrees will have no effect, as shown in the following code:

**skew**

```
#right{
    -webkit-transform: skew(0deg);
}
```

However, if we modify the code in the following manner:

```
#right{
    -webkit-transform: skewX(45deg);
}
```

We will see this in the web browser:

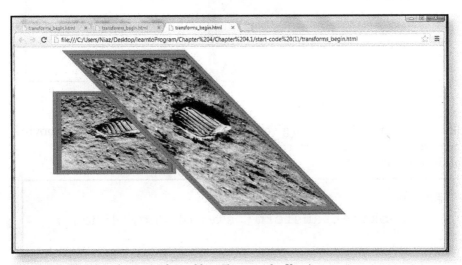

Figure 4.5: The right image is skewed by 45° across the X-axis.

Here we should carefully note that if we skew an object across the X-axis, the horizontal lines containing that object will not change their angle, but they will instead move left and right. Again, if we skew an object across the Y-axis, the vertical lines containing that object will not change their angle, but they will move up and down. So, if we change the code in this way:

```
#right{
    -webkit-transform: skewY(45deg);
}
```

Then we will see the following in our web browser:

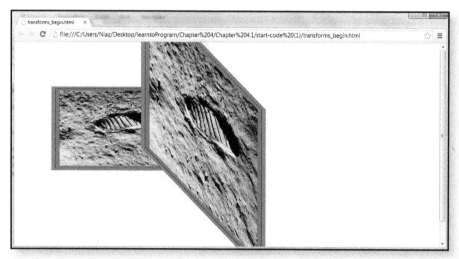

Figure 4.5: The right image is skewed by 45° across the Y-axis.

Skews are generally used to give the impression that the object is moving in three-dimensional space, so you may often see the skews in the following manner:

```
#right{
    -webkit-transform: skew(45deg, 45deg);
}
```

We can use the following code for our purpose:

```
#right{
    -webkit-transform: skew(45deg, 0deg);
}
```

The last *transform* property for us to look at is the *rotate* option. Let's apply this *rotate* rule to the body of our page, like this:

rotate

```
body{
-webkit-transform: rotate(15deg);
}
```

Here, we want to rotate all the elements by 15 degrees. In the browser, you will see this:

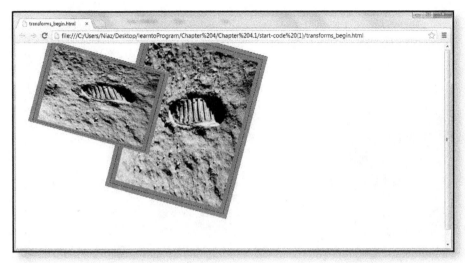

Figure 4.7: The images are rotated by 15°.

Now we are going to discuss transforms in three dimensions. Internet Explorer and Opera currently do not support 3-D transforming at all. So, if possible, it is highly recommended to use Google Chrome which will make it easier for you to follow the instructions given in this book. This is because Google Chrome currently supports most of the 3-D transform rules, but these are still not fully implemented. Let's get rid of all the transforms that we have used so far, and modify the code in this way:

```
#left{
    -webkit-transform: rotateY(30deg);
}

#left:hover{
}

#right{
-webkit-transform: rotateY(-30deg);
}

#right:hover{
}
```

Here we wanted to make sure that the images face each other to some degree. If we look at the browser, we will see this:

Figure 4.8: The rotate rule is not implemented, despite being mentioned in the code.

This is not what we expected. However, we can say that something has happened, as the images are shrunken horizontally, and there is a space between the two images. This is the specific limitation of the web browser in displaying 3-D elements. Let's go ahead and give the web browser viewing our page enough information about how our three-dimensional object should look to the viewer. We should use the *perspective* rule, and modify the code in the following manner:

**perspective**

```
#left{
-webkit-transform:
perspective(1000px) rotateY(30deg);
}

#left:hover{
}
```

```
#right{
-webkit-transform: perspective(1000px)
rotateY(-30deg);

}

#right:hover{
}
```

In the browser, we will see this:

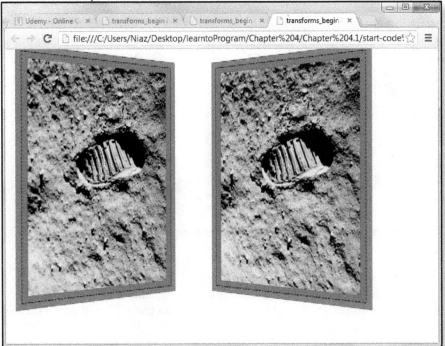

Figure 4.9: The two images are facing each other.

In the browser, you can see that the images are facing towards each other, and their inner edges are shorter than their outer edges, as we would expect of two three-dimensional pictures facing towards each other.

We can also declare the *perspective* rule outside of the transform rule, in an element which contains elements that have the transform rules, as shown here:

```
body{
-webkit-perspective: 1000px;
}
```

In the browser, we will see this:

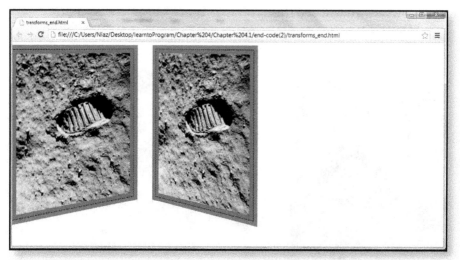

Figure 4.10: The images when perspective rule is declared outside of the element where the transform rule is declared.

Here we can see that the images are not actually the same, because we are looking from the center of our screen, and so the width of our left image appears larger.

It will probably be a little while before 3-D transforms are supported by all major web browsers. However, when they are fully implemented, we should be ready to use them in the way we want.

## QUESTIONS FOR REVIEW

1. Which action can't you perform by using the CSS transform rule?
   a. rotate
   b. scale
   c. skew
   d. animate

2. Which of the following options is used to move an image element?
   a. translate
   b. rotate
   c. scale
   d. skew

# 4.2 CSS3 Transitions

In this chapter we will learn about CSS3 **transitions**. *Transitions* allow us to describe functional, gradual state changes in objects. They are a very rudimentary form of animation.

Let's talk a little bit about this in-development CSS3 feature, CSS *transitions*. Currently not all browsers support it, for example, CSS3 transitions cannot be used in Internet Explorer. As a result, we have to be careful while choosing the browser where we will work.

Consider the following webpage:

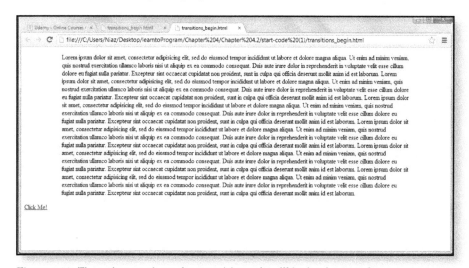

Figure 4.11: The webpage where the transition rule will be implemented.

Our goal in this chapter is to take the link at the bottom of the page and turn it into a very functional and useful element. We are going to remove it mostly from visibility on the webpage. We are going to turn it from an obvious weblink into a little tab that exists on the left of our page. When we put our mouse over this tab, we will see that it animates outwardly and the link is displayed in a manner that is pleasing to the eye.

Let's consider the corresponding HTML code:

## CODE LISTING: TRANSITIONS HTML

```
<!DOCTYPE html>
<html>
<head>
    <link rel="stylesheet" type="text/css"
href="transitions_end.css" />
</head>

<body>
    <p>
        Lorem ipsum dolor sit amet,
consectetur adipisicing elit, sed do eiusmod
tempor incididunt ut labore et dolore magna
aliqua. Ut enim ad minim veniam, quis
nostrud exercitation ullamco laboris nisi ut
aliquip ex ea commodo consequat. Duis aute
irure dolor in reprehenderit in voluptate
velit esse cillum dolore eu fugiat nulla
pariatur. Excepteur sint occaecat cupidatat
non proident, sunt in culpa qui officia
deserunt mollit anim id est laborum.
        Lorem ipsum dolor sit amet,
consectetur adipisicing elit, sed do eiusmod
tempor incididunt ut labore et dolore magna
aliqua. Ut enim ad minim veniam, quis
nostrud exercitation ullamco laboris nisi ut
aliquip ex ea commodo consequat. Duis aute
irure dolor in reprehenderit in voluptate
velit esse cillum dolore eu fugiat nulla
pariatur. Excepteur sint occaecat cupidatat
non proident, sunt in culpa qui officia
deserunt mollit anim id est laborum.
        Lorem ipsum ...........mollit anim id est
laborum.
        Lorem ipsum ...........mollit anim id est
```

```
laborum.
          Lorem ipsum ...........mollit anim id est
laborum.
          Lorem ipsum ...........mollit anim id est
laborum.
          Lorem ipsum ...........mollit anim id est
laborum.
          Lorem ipsum ...........mollit anim id est
laborum.
     </p>
     <a class="slider" href="transitions.
html">Click Me!</a>
     </body>
     </html>
```

Before we really need to call upon CSS3 transitions, we need to do some other CSS styling to our element to get it to behave in the way we have described. So, we have assigned a class to this element, and we have named it a 'slider' class. Now, let's see the corresponding CSS code:

## Code Listing: Transitions CSS

```
p{
    margin-left: 100px;
    margin-right: 100px;
}

.slider{
    top: 200px;

    position: absolute;
    left: 0px;
    height: 30px;
    line-height: 30px;

    width: 0px;
    overflow: hidden;
```

```
    padding-left: 15px;
    background-color: grey;

    border-top: black 2px solid;
    border-right: black 2px solid;
    border-bottom: black 2px solid;

    border-top-right-radius: 5px;
    -webkit-border-top-right-radius: 5px;
    border-bottom-right-radius: 5px;
    -webkit-border-bottom-right-radius: 5px;

    -webkit-transition: width 2s, background-
color 5.5s;
    -webkit-transition-timing-function:
linear;
}

.slider:hover{
    width: 80px;
    background-color: rgb(200,100,100);
}
```

In the browser, we will see this:

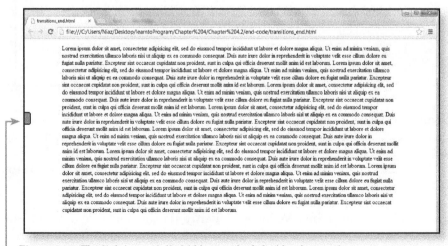

Figure 4.12: The link is partially hidden on the left side of our webpage

When we put our mouse over the link, we will see this:

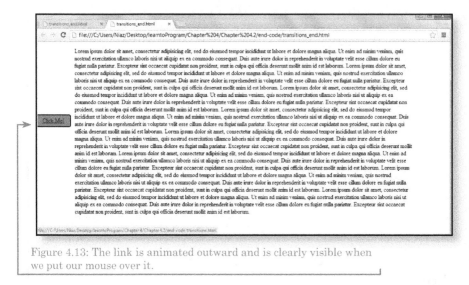

Figure 4.13: The link is animated outward and is clearly visible when
we put our mouse over it.

In this picture, you can see the effect of applying the *transition* rule to
the link, as it is animated outwardly and clearly visible. Let's analyze the
CSS code.

In order to position our element in the appropriate place, we have used
the following code:

```
.slider{
    top: 200px;

    position: absolute;
    left: 0px;
}
```

Having our link appear below all the text on the page is not convenient
for the user. Hence we have used *absolute* positioning, and if we combine
that with a 0 pixel left positioning, the element should appear on the
left-hand side of the page. We have also assigned a top positioning, so our
element is located 200 pixels from the top of the page.

In addition to positioning, we have explicitly set the height of our element
and have explicitly set the line-height, which is the height of the text on
our element, in this way:

```
.slider{
   top: 200px;

   position: absolute;
   left: 0px;
height: 30px;
   line-height: 30px;


}
```

We want the element in a hidden position, so we have used the following code:

```
width: 0px;
   overflow: hidden;
```

However, this will make the element completely invisible, which would make it difficult to locate so that we can put our mouse over it. To resolve this issue, we have used the following code:

```
padding-left: 15px;
   background-color: grey;
```

We have made one more cosmetic change to our element, which has made it look much more finalized and of higher quality. We have done it by adding a border around the element, using the following code:

```
border-top: black 2px solid;
   border-right: black 2px solid;
   border-bottom: black 2px solid;

   border-top-right-radius: 5px;
   -webkit-border-top-right-radius: 5px;
   border-bottom-right-radius: 5px;
   -webkit-border-bottom-right-radius: 5px;
```

Next, we have applied the *transition* property, using the following code:

```css
.slider{

-webkit-transition: width 2s, background-
color 5.5s;
    -webkit-transition-timing-function:
linear;
    }

.slider:hover{
    width: 80px;
    background-color: rgb(200,100,100);
}
```

In order to ensure that the link slides out from the side of the page rather than appearing immediately when we put the mouse over it, we have used the *transition* rule. CSS3 transitions allow us to create a number of steps in between two states.

Let's take a look at the syntax of the *transition* property. A CSS *transition* has two attributes. The first is the type of rule that we want this transition to apply across. In our case, we like to see a slow transition between widths for all 'slider' elements. The second one is how long we want the transition to go on, and we specify this in seconds. So, here, as our element changes width, it will create that change over the span of two seconds. Whenever we put our mouse over it, it goes through all the intermediate states between zero pixel width and 80 pixels width.

In order to ensure that the tab element that we have created pulls out from the left of the page at a steady speed, we have used the following code:

```css
-webkit-transition-timing-function: linear;
```

If instead we used the following:

```css
-webkit-transition-timing-function: ease;
```

Then the transition would occur slowly at first, then quickly in the middle, and then again slowly at the end.

We also wanted to change the background color of our link, so we used the following code:

```
.slider:hover{
    width: 80px;
    background-color: rgb(200,100,100);
}
```

This would cause the background color of the link to change instantaneously when we hovered over it. If we wanted our background color to change gradually over time, we could use the following:

```
.slider{

-webkit-transition: width 2s, background-
color 5.5s;
    }
```

This will ensure that the background color changes slowly, over the course of 5.5 seconds.

You should now be fairly comfortable with CSS3 transitions, which can make your webpages look professional and polished. They allow you to add some dynamic functionality without using an additional language like Javascript.

QUESTIONS FOR REVIEW

1. Which web browser can CSS3 transforms not be used in?
   a. Google Chrome.
   b. Internet Explorer.
   c. Opera.
   d. Mozilla Firefox.

2. How many attributes do CSS transitions have?
   a. One.
   b. Two.
   c. Three.
   d. Four.

# 4.3 CSS3 ANIMATIONS

CSS3 allows us to apply animations to our HTML objects. In this chapter we will take a look at how it is done. Before beginning, you should know that Internet Explorer currently does not support CSS3 animations. So, if you want to follow along with the things mentioned in this chapter, you will have to use other major web browsers, like Google Chrome or Mozilla Firefox.

CSS3 animations are very powerful. Like transitions, animations allow us to describe how an HTML element changes from one state to another. Unlike transitions, animations also allow us to specify what these states are going to be.

In order to see what this means, let's begin by adding a very simple animation to our page. Our page currently contains a simple paragraph element, as shown in the following code:

```
<!DOCTYPE html>
<html>
<head>
    <link rel="stylesheet" type="text/css"
href="animations_begin.css" />
</head>

<body>
    <p>I am animated! I am animated! I am
animated! I am animated! I am animated!</p>
</body>
</html>

Let's also take a look at the corresponding
CSS code:

p{
    width: 100px;
    height: 100px;
    background-color:red;
}
```

In the browser, we will see the following:

Figure 4.14: The webpage with a single element.

Let's create our first animation! We'll have the background color of this paragraph change from red to blue, over the course of a couple of seconds. Even though we are assigning an animation to this paragraph element, we are going to define how our animation operates in a separate CSS rule. Then we are going to place that defined animation within the rule of the paragraph selector. This allows us to attribute a single animation to multiple different types of elements which share similar starting conditions.

CSS3 considers animations as a series of keyframes. Each keyframe is a state that we want our object to pass through over the course of its animation. Now, we are going to define all of the keyframes that we are going to use. We do this in a separate rule (termed an "at rule"), prefaced with the @ symbol, and the keyword will be *keyframes,* as shown in the following code:

## CODE LISTING: ANIMATED COLOR BOX CSS

```
p{
    width: 100px;
    height: 100px;
    background-color:red;
```

```
    -webkit-animation: colorChange 4s;
}

@-webkit-keyframes colorChange{
    from {background-color: red;}
    to {background-color: blue;}
}
```

W3C recommends that all animations explicitly declare a *from* or 0% keyframe, defining all of our assumptions at the start of the animation. So, we have defined in our *from* keyframe our only assumption, and that is, the element that we are animating has a background color of red. Then the only other thing that we need to do in the keyframes of our animation is to declare how the element should look at the very end of its animation. We have decided that at the end of the animation, or at 100%, we would like the background color of our element to be blue. Again, in order to assign these keyframes to the animation for our paragraph element, we have used the name 'colorChange', and we have selected four seconds as the duration of our animation. In the web browser, you will see that our paragraph element transitions from red to blue, as shown here:

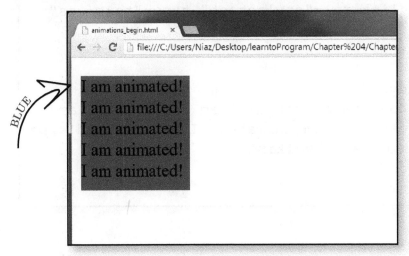

Figure 4.15: Here, the element has transitioned from red to blue. However, after four seconds, when the animation is complete, the element transitions back to its default state.

To explore the intricacies of CSS3 animations, let's create a more complicated animation. For this second animation, we are going to use a spritesheet to make a character walk back and forth across our screen indefinitely. So, in this chapter, we are going to use the *window* method of sprite creation. We will use the following two images:

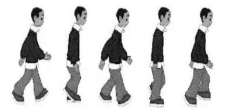

Figure 4.16: walking.png

Figure 4.17: The transparent image

Here, the transparent image defines the width and height of each frame of our little walking man. Before we animate any object, we need to add it to our page, like this:

## CODE LISTING: ANIMATIONS HTML

```
<!DOCTYPE html>
<html>
<head>
    <link rel="stylesheet" type="text/css"
href="animations_end.css" />
</head>

<body>
    <p>I am animated! I am animated! I am
animated! I am animated! I am animated!</p>
    <img src="walking.png"/>
</body>
</html>
```

Let's add the following CSS code:

## CODE LISTING: ANIMATED SPRITE CSS

```css
img{
    background-image: url("walking.png");
    position: relative;

    -webkit-animation: walk 1s, move 20s;
    -webkit-animation-iteration-count:
infinite;
    -webkit-animation-timing-function: step-
start, linear;
}

@-webkit-keyframes walk{
    0% {background-position: 0;}
    25% {background-position: -19px}
    50% {background-position: -38px;}
    75% {background-position: -57px;}
    100% {background-position: 0;}
}

@-webkit-keyframes move{
    0% {left: 0; -webkit-transform:
scaleX(1);}
    50% {left: 100%; -webkit-transform:
scaleX(1);}
    51% {left: 100%; -webkit-transform:
scaleX(-1);}
    100% {left: 0; -webkit-transform:
scaleX(-1);}
}
```

In the browser, we will see that the image moves back and forth across our webpage continuously, as shown below:

Figure 4.18: The image moves back and forth across our webpage.

Let's analyze the code. We have set up another list of keyframes, and have defined five different keyframes of animation. The reason for this is because we want our animation to end in the same state that it began, so that we can loop the animation over and over again, without making any jumps.

In order to confirm what our element will look like in each keyframe, we have used the following code:

```
@-webkit-keyframes walk{
    0% {background-position: 0;}
    25% {background-position: -19px}
    50% {background-position: -38px;}
    75% {background-position: -57px;}
    100% {background-position: 0;}
}
```

For each of our frames of animation, we want to change the background position by 19 pixels. At the very end, when our animation has completed a run-through, we want it to be back at the very beginning, the first image we saw, so that it will smoothly transition to another run-through.

We have also assigned our animation to our image, which is the 'walk' animation, and let's have it occur over the course of one second, like this:

```
-webkit-animation: walk 1s;
```

To create an animation that loops over and over, we use the following code:

```
-webkit-animation-iteration-count: infinite;
```

In order to ensure that our animation jumps from one defined keyframe to another without hitting the steps in between, we have used this:

```
-webkit-animation-timing-function: step-start;
```

To ensure that our image moves indefinitely across our webpage, we have created a separate set of keyframes, as shown here:

```
@-webkit-keyframes move{
    0% {left: 0; -webkit-transform:
scaleX(1);}
    50% {left: 100%; -webkit-transform:
scaleX(1);}
    51% {left: 100%; -webkit-transform:
scaleX(-1);}
    100% {left: 0; -webkit-transform:
scaleX(-1);}
    }
```

The 50% keyframe is halfway through our animation, and so when the animation is 50% completed, our image element will be on the very right-hand side of the containing element, which is the body of our page. Then, we want our animation to end on the very left-hand side of our page.

The other thing we need to do is flip our element, since it is facing the wrong direction while moving from left to right. We'll do that using the *transform* property, in the following manner:

```
-webkit-transform: scaleX(-1);
```

We have also made some other necessary modifications in the code, which are shown here:

```
img {

-webkit-animation: walk 1s, move 20s;
-webkit-animation-timing-function: step-
start, linear;
}
```

This will ensure that our *move* animation occurs in linear time.

Prior to CSS3 animations, we really had to rely on languages like Javascript to create these visually appealing effects on our webpages. It is W3C's hope that adding this powerful animation support to CSS will reduce our need to rely on other languages.

 QUESTIONS FOR REVIEW

1. CSS3 animations cannot be used in which web browser?
   a. Internet Explorer.
   b. Google Chrome.
   c. Opera.
   d. Mozilla Firefox.

2. The code to define all of the keyframes is prefaced with which symbol?
   a. #
   b. @
   c. &
   d. !

# CHAPTER 4 LAB EXERCISE

Consider the following HTML code:

```
<!DOCTYPE html>
<html>
<head>
    <link rel="stylesheet" type="text/css"
href="LabStart.css" />
</head>

<body>
    <div id="container">
        <div id="anim-target"></div>
    </div>
</body>
</html>
```

And also consider the corresponding CSS
code:

```
#container{
    width: 500px;
    height: 500px;
    outline: 2px solid black;
}

#anim-target{
    width: 50px;
    height: 50px;
    background-color: red;
}
```

Employ a browser other than Internet Explorer for this exercise.

Modify the CSS file so that the red box will grow to fill its containing element when moused over.

Remove the height and width from the red box. Write new CSS so that the containing <div> fills with red when it is moused over. Can you get your element to fill from a side, rather than the top left corner?

Add a *body:active* rule to your CSS. In this rule, combine a 3DTransform and a Transition to cause your page to spin around its Y axis when the mouse is held down. (Hint: Due to browser implementations, do not use the short-hand *transition:* rule, use *transition-duration:* and *transition-property:* on separate lines.)

Finally, return the width and height of the red <div> to 50px. Apply an animation to this <div> so that it moves perpetually along the inside four corners of its container. (Hint: *position:relative*)

# CHAPTER 4 LAB SOLUTIONS

## LAB SOLUTION HTML

```
<!DOCTYPE html>
<html>
<head>
    <link rel="stylesheet" type="text/css"
href="LabSolution.css" />
</head>

<body>
    <div id="container">
        <div id="anim-target"></div>
    </div>
</body>
</html>
```

## LAB SOLUTION CSS

```
#container{
    width: 500px;
    height: 500px;
    outline: 2px solid black;
}

/*For an anim-target which grows to the size of
its container when moused over...*/
/*
#anim-target{
    transition: width 2s, height 2s;
    -moz-transition: width 2s, height 2s;
    -webkit-transition: width 2s, height 2s;
    -o-transition: width 2s, height 2s;

    width: 50px;
    height: 50px;
    background-color: red;
}

#anim-target:hover{
    width: 100%;
    height: 100%;
}
*/

/*For a container which will fill with color
when moused over...*/
/*
#anim-target{
    transition: width 2s, height 2s;
    -moz-transition: width 2s, height 2s;
    -webkit-transition: width 2s, height 2s;
    -o-transition: width 2s, height 2s;

    float: right;
    height: 100%;
```

```css
    width: 0;
    background-color: red;
}
*:hover>#anim-target{
    width: 100%;
    height: 100%;
}
*/

/*To make a page that rotates while the mouse
is held down...*/
/*
body:active{
    transform: rotateY(360deg);
    transition-property: rotate 5s;
    transition-duration: 5s;
    -moz-transform: rotateY(360deg);
    -moz-transition-property: rotate 5s;
    -moz-transition-duration: 5s;
    -webkit-transform: rotateY(360deg);
    -webkit-transition-property: rotate 5s;
    -webkit-transition-duration: 5s;
    -o-transform: rotateY(360deg);
    -o-transition-property: rotate 5s;
    -o-transition-duration: 5s;
}
*/

/*A moving red block...*/
#anim-target{
    width: 50px;
    height: 50px;
    background-color: red;

    position: relative;
    animation: anim 10s infinite;
    -moz-animation: anim 10s infinite;
    -webkit-animation: anim 10s infinite;
    -o-animation: anim 10s infinite;
}

    @keyframes anim{
```

```
        0%{top:0; left:0;}
        25%{top:0; left:450px;}
        50%{top:450px; left:450px;}
        75%{top:450px; left:0;}
        100%{top:0; left:0;}
}
@-moz-keyframes anim{
        0%{top:0; left:0;}
        25%{top:0; left:450px;}
        50%{top:450px; left:450px;}
        75%{top:450px; left:0;}
        100%{top:0; left:0;}
}
@-webkit-keyframes anim{
        0%{top:0; left:0;}
        25%{top:0; left:450px;}
        50%{top:450px; left:450px;}
        75%{top:450px; left:0;}
        100%{top:0; left:0;}
}
@-o-keyframes anim{
        0%{top:0; left:0;}
        25%{top:0; left:450px;}
        50%{top:450px; left:450px;}
        75%{top:450px; left:0;}
        100%{top:0; left:0;}
}
```

# CHAPTER 4 SUMMARY

In this chapter we learned how to use CSS transforms. We have realized how we can easily translate, scale, rotate, and skew an element using CSS3.

We have also gained hands-on experience regarding using CSS3 transforms. We have clarified how to use this rudimentary form of animations using CSS3.

We have explored the use of CSS3 animations in different manners. We have understood that, in order to do animations on a webpage successfully, CSS3 will be enough—we will not have to resort to other languages like Javascript.

In the next chapter, we will discuss block and inline elements, and also the effects of changing around the display attribute of our elements. We will also learn the options available when it comes to positioning elements.

# CHAPTER 5
## PUTTING ELEMENTS TOGETHER

### CHAPTER OBJECTIVES:

- You will understand the role of *block* and *inline* elements in HTML when it comes to styling the webpage.
- You will learn the effects of changing the *display* property of elements.
- You will understand the options that you have when it comes to positioning elements.
- You will learn how to use the *float* attribute to position the elements.

## 5.1 THE DISPLAY PROPERTY

Nothing turns CSS into a frustration faster than when the elements on our page don't appear the way we expect them to. In this chapter, we will be taking a look at the CSS **display** property, which allows us to choose how our webpage elements arrange and order themselves on the screen. Let's begin by taking a look at the page we are going to be modifying:

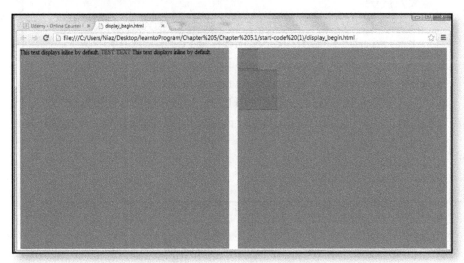

Figure 5.1: The webpage with two different sections.

As you can see, we have divided the page into two sections for our convenience: two grey boxes. For the purposes of this chapter, these boxes should always act independently. We have also done some basic visual styling inline in our HTML code, so that we can keep the CSS code that we are going to be modifying very clean and simple, as shown here:

## CODE LISTING: DISPLAY HTML

```html
<!DOCTYPE html>
<html>
<head>
    <link rel="stylesheet" type="text/css"
href="display_begin.css" />
</head>

<body>
    <div style="width: 49%; height: 500px;
float: left; background-color: grey;">
        <span>This text displays inline by
default.</span>
        <span id="col1">TEST TEXT</span>
        <span>This text displays inline by
default.</span>
    </div>
    <div style="width:49%; height: 500px;
float: right; background-color: grey;">
        <div class="col2" style="width:
50px; height: 50px; margin: 2px;"></div>
        <div class="col2" style="width:
100px; height: 100px; margin: 2px;"></div>
    </div>
</body>
</html>
```

Let's also take a look at the corresponding CSS code:

## CODE LISTING: DISPLAY CSS

```
#col1{
    color: blue;
    display:inline;
}

.col2{
    background-color: red;
    display: block;
}
```

Here you can see that we have two CSS rules. The first rule, the col1 *ID* selector, refers to the blue text on the left section of our page. This is a **span** element, contained between two other *span* elements. We also have a **class** selector, which refers to both of the two red boxes on the right section. These are both **div** elements, which we have given different widths and heights.

In addition to some basic color styling, you can see that we have explicitly assigned values to the *display* properties for all of our elements in the CSS code. Currently, these rules are unnecessary. Our *span* elements would have defaulted to *inline* display anyway, and our *div* elements would also have defaulted to the *block* display. So, if we remove both of these rules, our page would not change.

*span* **elements** default to *inline* **display.**

*div* **elements** default to *block* **display.**

Let's take a look at the difference in behavior between the elements displaying *inline* on our left and the elements displaying *block* on our right. The most obvious difference is that the elements on our left are allowed to group horizontally. The elements begin one after another, and the third span element wraps down to the second line once the content area of the containing box is reached.

Again, on the right side, it certainly seems that the second larger *div* element could have appeared on the right of the smaller *div*, but it chose not to. When our browser begins rendering elements displaying *block*, like these elements, it begins by jumping down to a new line, and then when it finishes displaying a *block* element, it creates another new line. This causes the *block* elements to not tolerate elements on the same horizontal axis.

Let's take another look at the elements displaying *inline* on the left. An important thing that needs to be mentioned is that a line can be of any height, and this depends on the height of the largest element it's required to contain. A line will continue displaying the elements within it until it reaches the end of the content area that is allowed, and then a new line will appear beneath, and the elements will continue to display, as shown in figure 5.2.

If we were to add some more *span* elements to our code in the following manner:

```
<!DOCTYPE html>
<html>
<head>
    <link rel="stylesheet" type="text/css"
href="display_begin.css" />
</head>

<body>
    <div style="width: 49%; height: 500px;
float: left; background-color: grey;">
    <span>This text displays inline by
default.</span>
    <span id="col1">TEST TEXT</span>
    <span>This text displays inline by
default.</span>
    <span>This text displays inline by
default.</span>
    <span>This text displays inline by
default.</span>
    <span>This text displays inline by
default.</span>
    <span>This text displays inline by
default.</span>
    <span>This text displays inline by
default.</span>
```

```
</div>

<div style="width:49%; height: 500px; float:
right; background-color: grey;">
    <div class="col2" style="width: 50px;
height: 50px; margin: 2px;"></div>
    <div class="col2" style="width: 100px;
height: 100px; margin: 2px;"></div>
    </div>
</body>
</html>
```

Then in the browser, we will see this:

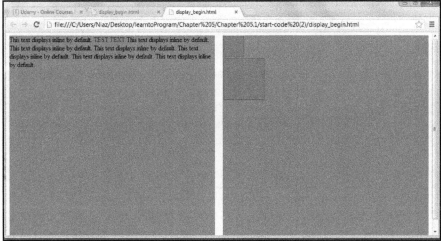

Figure 5.2: More *span* elements are added on the left section.

Now, if we increase the *line-height* of our element to 50 pixels in the CSS code, like this:

```
#col1{
    color: blue;
    display:inline;
    line-height: 50px;

}
```

Then we will see the following change in our webpage:

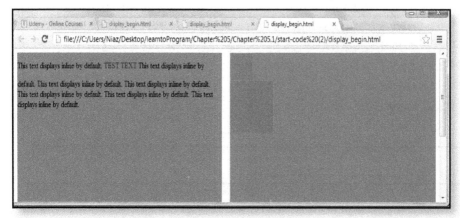

Figure 5.3: The span elements on the left section after the line-height is increased.

Here you can see that the distance between the elements in the first two lines has increased, and this has happened despite the fact that the *line-height* of only a single span element is increased in the first line. As we have declared that the *line-height* of the element will be 50 pixels, all of the elements belonging to that line must adhere to that rule.

Let's change the display property of these elements, like this:

```
#col1{
    color: blue;
    display:block;
}

.col2{
    background-color: red;
    display: inline;
}
```

In the browser, we will see the following change:

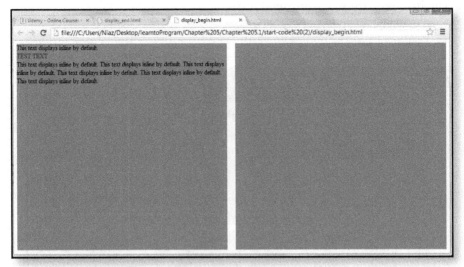

Figure 5.4: The webpage after changing the display property of the elements.

Let's begin with the spans. As we know, block elements force new lines at their beginning and end, so that they don't display horizontally next to any other elements. By declaring that the particular span element displays as a block, we force it to separate out the rest of the spans into two groups: those above it, (which are the ones before it) and those below it (which is everything that comes after).

More dramatically, our *div* elements have disappeared. That's because they are now displaying within a line, and as we know, the height of a line is the height of the largest content it needs to contain. Our *div* elements have declared heights, which allowed us to see their background color when they were displaying *block*. However, when the elements are displayed *inline*, the heights we have assigned to them don't matter, only the height of the line that contains them does. So, our divs have essentially been reduced to the height of the line containing them, which is zero.

If we want our divs to display next to each other, left and right, like our *inline* spans did, we have to set their *display* property to **inline-block**:

```
.col2{
    background-color: red;
    display: inline-block;
}
```

In the browser, we will see this:

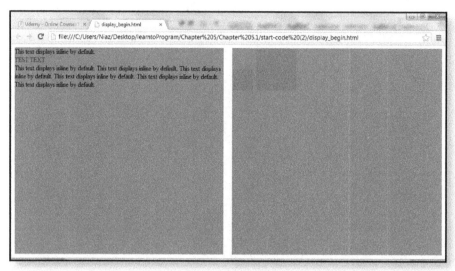

Figure 5.5: The *div* elements are displayed on the right section, side-by-side.

The *inline-block* property value causes a line to form around our block elements, which is large enough to contain the largest block element, and then it allows the elements to display horizontally next to each other by not forcing new lines.

Making good use of the *display* property when we are setting up a webpage is important. The *inline, block* or *inline-block* property values describe the basic setup of our page. The more accurately we describe how we want the elements to display with the *display* property, the less direct positioning we are going to have to do to those elements later.

**Display Property**
→ inline
→ block
→ inline-block

We like to think of the *display* property as our first step towards getting our page's elements outlined in the way we want them. Rather than putting an element in a very specific position, we are simply telling the CSS what kind of element we are creating at this point of time.

## QUESTIONS FOR REVIEW

1. Which type of elements force new lines at their beginning and end?
   a. block
   b. span
   c. vertical
   d. None of the above.

2. Which *display* property is used when we want the *block* elements to ignore the forcing of new lines at their beginning and end?
   a. inline
   b. block
   c. inline-block
   d. None of the above.

# 5.2 In-Depth CSS Positioning

In this section, we will take a look at the intricacies of the CSS *position* property, which tells our elements how they are going to be displayed on our webpage. It works closely with the *top, bottom, left,* and *right* properties and the *center* property value. Let's take a quick look at the webpage that we are going to be modifying:

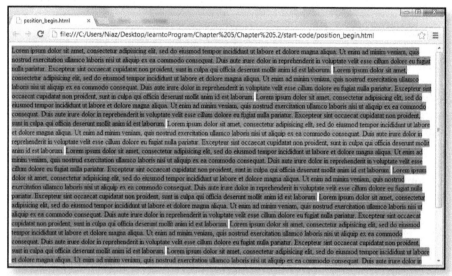

Figure 5.6: The webpage with text elements (highlighted purple) that will be modified in this chapter.

Let's see the corresponding HTML Code:

## CODE LISTING: POSITIONING HTML

```
<!DOCTYPE html>
<html>
<head>
    <link rel="stylesheet" type="text/css"
href="position_begin.css" />
</head>

<body>
    <span class="show-bkg">Lorem ipsum dolor
sit amet, consectetur adipisicing elit, sed do
```

*CSS Development (with CSS3!)*

eiusmod tempor incididunt ut labore et dolore magna aliqua. Ut enim ad minim veniam, quis nostrud exercitation ullamco laboris nisi ut aliquip ex ea commodo consequat. Duis aute irure dolor in reprehenderit in voluptate velit esse cillum dolore eu fugiat nulla pariatur. Excepteur sint occaecat cupidatat non proident, sunt in culpa qui officia deserunt mollit anim id est laborum.</span>

    <span class="show-bkg">Lorem ipsum dolor sit amet, consectetur adipisicing elit, sed do eiusmod tempor incididunt ut labore et dolore magna aliqua. Ut enim ad minim veniam, quis nostrud exercitation ullamco laboris nisi ut aliquip ex ea commodo consequat. Duis aute irure dolor in reprehenderit in voluptate velit esse cillum dolore eu fugiat nulla pariatur. Excepteur sint occaecat cupidatat non proident, sunt in culpa qui officia deserunt mollit anim id est laborum.</span>

    <span class="show-bkg">Lorem ipsum dolor sit amet, consectetur adipisicing elit, sed do eiusmod tempor incididunt ut labore et dolore magna aliqua. Ut enim ad minim veniam, quis nostrud exercitation ullamco laboris nisi ut aliquip ex ea commodo consequat. Duis aute irure dolor in reprehenderit in voluptate velit esse cillum dolore eu fugiat nulla pariatur. Excepteur sint occaecat cupidatat non proident, sunt in culpa qui officia deserunt mollit anim id est laborum.</span>

    <span id="target">Lorem ipsum dolor sit amet, consectetur adipisicing elit, sed do eiusmod tempor incididunt ut labore et dolore magna aliqua. Ut enim ad minim veniam, quis nostrud exercitation ullamco laboris nisi ut aliquip ex ea commodo consequat. Duis aute irure dolor in reprehenderit in voluptate velit esse cillum dolore eu fugiat nulla pariatur. Excepteur sint occaecat cupidatat non proident, sunt in culpa qui officia deserunt mollit anim

```
id est laborum.</span>
    <span class="show-bkg">Lorem ipsum dolor
sit amet, consectetur adipisicing elit, sed do
eiusmod tempor incididunt ut labore et dolore
magna aliqua. Ut enim ad minim veniam, quis
nostrud exercitation ullamco laboris nisi ut
aliquip ex ea commodo consequat. Duis aute
irure dolor in reprehenderit in voluptate velit
esse cillum dolore eu fugiat nulla pariatur.
Excepteur sint occaecat cupidatat non proident,
sunt in culpa qui officia deserunt mollit anim
id est laborum.</span>
    <span class="show-bkg">Lorem ipsum ...............</
span>
    <span class="show-bkg">Lorem ipsum ...............</
span>
    <span class="show-bkg">Lorem ipsum ...............</
span>
    <span class="show-bkg">Lorem ipsum ...............</
span>
    <span class="show-bkg">Lorem ipsum ...............</
span>
    <span class="show-bkg">Lorem ipsum ...............</
span>
</body>
</html>
```

We can also take a look at the CSS code:

## CODE LISTING: POSITIONING CSS

```
.show-bkg{
    background-color: grey;
}

#target{
    background-color: rgb(150,150,255);
    position: static;
}
```

We are going to be assigning different positioning values to the blue highlighted *span* element, which is among many other spans on our webpage. You can see in the CSS code that we have assigned this span with blue highlight a *position* value of **static**. This is the default value for just about every HTML element. *Static* positioning means that this element, along with all the other *span* elements on our page, will display according to what we call **normal flow**. They are all line elements, so they simply follow the rule of line element display, starting from the top-left of our content area, and ending at the bottom-right corner. The important thing to realize about static positioned elements is that they disable our ability to offset their position with the *top, bottom, left,* and *right* style propeties, or the *center* property value. If we specify a *top* offset of 100 pixels, in the following manner:

**Position Property**

→ static
→ fixed
→ relative
→ absolute

**static**

```
#target{
    background-color: rgb(150,150,255);

    top: 100px;
    position: static;
}
```

Then we will see that no changes will occur, because this *static* position rule explicitly says that this element will be positioned based on the normal flow.

Let's take a look at this behavior from our conceptual viewpoint. Why would elements with their *position* property set to *static* not do anything when we attempt this offset of 100 elements? This implementation decision was made because offsets are going to have different behaviors based on what position option we choose. For instance, if we set the *position* property to *relative*, in this way:

**relative**

```
#target{
    background-color: rgb(150,150,255);

    top: 100px;
    position: relative;
}
```

Then our element is going to display 100 pixels below where it would have normally. We have moved the element 100 pixels from its original top, as shown here:

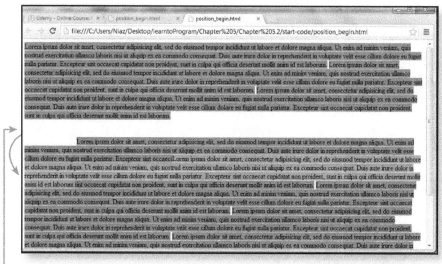

Figure 5.7: The element has moved 100 pixels down from its original position.

The important thing to notice here is that the area the element originally occupied is still physically occupied. We have only moved the visual portion of the element. Physically, it still displays in normal flow.

However, we get significantly different results if we set the *position* property to *absolute*, as shown here:

**absolute**

```
#target{
    background-color: rgb(150,150,255);

    top: 100px;
    position: absolute;
}
```

In the browser, we will see this:

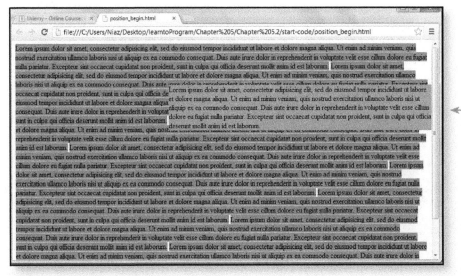

Figure 5.8: The position of the element is changed after using *absolute* positioning.

You can see here that our element appears floating in a different position, and the physical space that it originally occupied is gone. This tells us that positioning an element *absolutely* does two things. First, our offset is no longer in terms of where the element was originally. If it was, we would expect our element to display somewhere around the middle part of the page. Rather, it's displaying 100 pixels from the top of our page; or more specifically, it is displaying 100 pixels from the top of its containing element, or the body of the page. We can see this clearly if we change its top to zero, like this:

```
#target{
    background-color: rgb(150,150,255);

    top: 0;
    position: absolute;
}
```

We will see this in the browser:

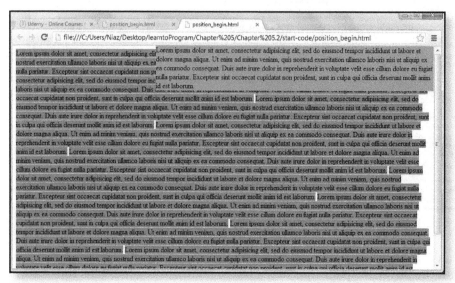

Figure 5.9: The position of the element is changed, now at the top of the page.

The other important thing that *absolute* positioning of this element did was to physically take the element out of the normal flow. So, the space that it used to occupy now no longer exists.

This is similar to what would happen if we set the position property to *fixed*. We can use it as shown here:

**fixed**

```
#target{
    background-color: rgb(150,150,255);

    top: 0;
    position: fixed;
}
```

In the browser, we will see this:

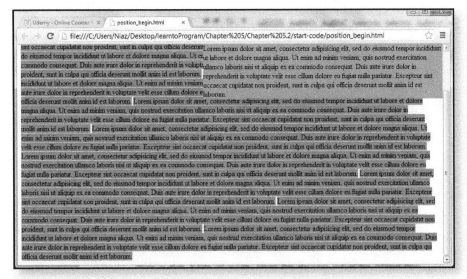

Figure 5.10: The position of the element is fixed at the top.

At first, it appears that nothing has changed. However, when we scroll down this page, we can observe that our element remains fixed where it was before, at the top of the page. Whereas the position *relative* places an element in terms of its container, which for our purpose here is the body of the page; position *fixed* places an element in terms of the view of the browser.

We can also declare position offsets in terms of a percentage, in this way:

```
#target{
    background-color: rgb(150,150,255);

    top: 50%;
    position: fixed;
}
```

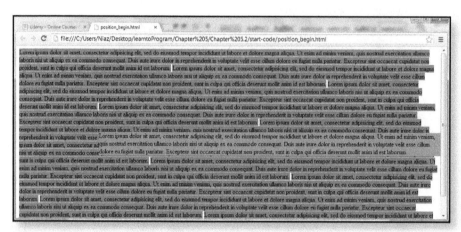

Figure 5.11: The position of the element when offset of 50% at the top is selected.

A 50% *top* offset indicates that the top of our element is 50% of the way between the top and the bottom of its containing element, which is not the page itself, but it is our browser viewpoint currently. *Left* and *right* offset work in the same way.

Let's discuss an offset-like property, called the **z-index**. *Z-index* allows us to declare when elements should display in front of or behind other elements. If we set the *z-index* value to -1, as shown here:

```
#target{
    background-color: rgb(150,150,255);

    top: 50%;
    z-index=-1;
    position: fixed;
}
```

We will see this:

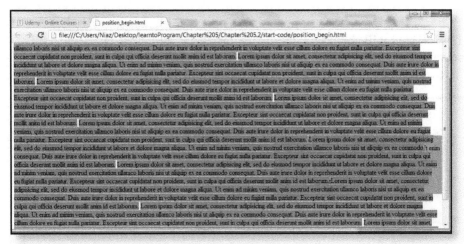

Figure 5.12: The element goes behind the other elements because of the negative value of the *z-index*.

Here you can see that our element goes behind the other elements. This becomes evident when we move the scroll bar of our webpage. On the other hand, a positive value of *z-index* will bring the element in front of other elements.

By the end of this chapter you should feel very comfortable with positions and how they affect your offset rules. Using positioning and offsets, we can really get the elements on our page to appear anywhere we want them to. Remember though, before you aggressively position your elements, do your very best to get your page looking generally how you want it to look using the simpler and less-intrusive options of *inline* and *block* styling.

## QUESTIONS FOR REVIEW

1. How many offset rules are there?
   - a. Two.
   - b. Three.
   - c. Four.
   - d. Five.

2. What is the default position of the span elements of our page?
   - a. static
   - b. fixed
   - c. absolute
   - d. relative

# 5.3 FLOATING ELEMENTS

This section will cover the CSS **float** property, which we can use to fill some gaps in the functionality of the *display* and *position* properties. Let's take a look at the page we are going to be editing:

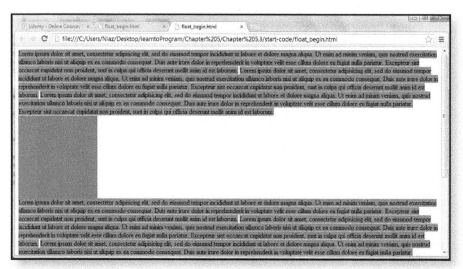

Figure 5.13: The webpage with *span* and *div* elements. The block in between appears red.

This page primarily consists of *span* elements: all the text on the page. Because they are *span* elements, we know that they have defaulted to *inline* display. We also have a red box on our page, which is simply a *div* element with a fixed width and height, and of course a background color so that we can see it. As a *div*, this element has defaulted to *block* display—that's where the line breaks before and after the *div* come from.

Let's see the corresponding HTML code:

## CODE LISTING: FLOAT ELEMENT HTML

```
<!DOCTYPE html>
<html>
<head>
    <link rel="stylesheet" type="text/css"
href="float_begin.css" />
</head>

<body>
```

```
    <span class="show-bkg">Lorem ipsum dolor
sit amet, consectetur adipisicing elit, sed do
eiusmod tempor incididunt ut labore et dolore
magna aliqua. Ut enim ad minim veniam, quis
nostrud exercitation ullamco laboris nisi ut
aliquip ex ea commodo consequat. Duis aute
irure dolor in reprehenderit in voluptate velit
esse cillum dolore eu fugiat nulla pariatur.
Excepteur sint occaecat cupidatat non proident,
sunt in culpa qui officia deserunt mollit anim
id est laborum.</span>
    <span class="show-bkg">Lorem ipsum dolor
sit amet, consectetur adipisicing elit, sed do
eiusmod tempor incididunt ut labore et dolore
magna aliqua. Ut enim ad minim veniam, quis
nostrud exercitation ullamco laboris nisi ut
aliquip ex ea commodo consequat. Duis aute
irure dolor in reprehenderit in voluptate velit
esse cillum dolore eu fugiat nulla pariatur.
Excepteur sint occaecat cupidatat non proident,
sunt in culpa qui officia deserunt mollit anim
id est laborum.</span>
    <span class="show-bkg">Lorem ipsum dolor
sit amet, consectetur adipisicing elit, sed do
eiusmod tempor incididunt ut labore et dolore
magna aliqua. Ut enim ad minim veniam, quis
nostrud exercitation ullamco laboris nisi ut
aliquip ex ea commodo consequat. Duis aute
irure dolor in reprehenderit in voluptate velit
esse cillum dolore eu fugiat nulla pariatur.
Excepteur sint occaecat cupidatat non proident,
sunt in culpa qui officia deserunt mollit anim
id est laborum.</span>
    <div id="target-left"></div>
    <span class="show-bkg">Lorem ipsum dolor
sit amet, consectetur adipisicing elit, sed do
eiusmod tempor incididunt ut labore et dolore
magna aliqua. Ut enim ad minim veniam, quis
nostrud exercitation ullamco laboris nisi ut
aliquip ex ea commodo consequat. Duis aute
irure dolor in reprehenderit in voluptate velit
```

```
esse cillum dolore eu fugiat nulla pariatur.
Excepteur sint occaecat cupidatat non proident,
sunt in culpa qui officia deserunt mollit anim
id est laborum.</span>
    <span class="show-bkg">Lorem ipsum dolor
sit amet, consectetur adipisicing elit, sed do
eiusmod tempor incididunt ut labore et dolore
magna aliqua. Ut enim ad minim veniam, quis
nostrud exercitation ullamco laboris nisi ut
aliquip ex ea commodo consequat. Duis aute
irure dolor in reprehenderit in voluptate velit
esse cillum dolore eu fugiat nulla pariatur.
Excepteur sint occaecat cupidatat non proident,
sunt in culpa qui officia deserunt mollit anim
id est laborum.</span>
    <span class="show-bkg">Lorem ipsum.........
laborum.</span>
    <span class="show-bkg"> Lorem ipsum.........
laborum.</span>    <span class="show-
bkg"> Lorem ipsum.........laborum.</span> <span
class="show-bkg"> Lorem ipsum.........laborum.</
span>    <span class="show-bkg"> Lorem ipsum.........
laborum.</span>    <span class="show-bkg">
Lorem ipsum.........laborum.</span>
</body>
</html>
```

And the CSS code:

CODE LISTING: FLOAT ELEMENT CSS

```
.show-bkg{
    background-color: grey;
}

#target-left{
    background-color: red;

    width: 200px;
```

```
    height: 200px;

}
```

Our goal here is to modify this webpage so that our red box displays in what appears to be the general flow of the page. We want to remove the unnecessary white space and have our text occupy all the blank spaces of the page.

You can probably guess that we are going to use the CSS *float* property to do this. But first, let's look at our options using *positioning* and *display* tags to see the necessity of using the *float* property.

In the CSS code, we have assigned the *target-left* id selector to our *div* element, which is the red box. Let's begin by attempting to achieve our styling goals of getting rid of all that white space created by placing a block element in the middle of the text, by simply using the *display* property, like this:

```
#target-left{
    background-color: red;

    width: 200px;
    height: 200px;

    display: block;
}
```

Because we are working with a *div* element, we know that we have defaulted to display *block*, and this will give us a large section of whitespace created by the line-breaks placed in the beginning and after the block element. Hence, this will not serve our purpose at all, and the result will be the same.

We also know that if we use the *inline* option in this way:

```
#target-left{
    background-color: red;

    width: 200px;
    height: 200px;
```

```
    display: inline;
}
```

Then our *div* will disappear, because of the zero *line-height*. So, this is not the correct option either.

We have solved similar issues in the previous chapter by using *inline-block* display property value. We can use it here:

```
display: inline-block;
```

In the browser, we will observe the following:

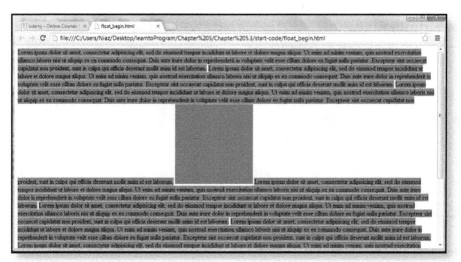

Figure 5.14: The position of the *div* element is changed after using the *inline-block* display property.

What's happened here is that all of our spans up to the *div* have been displayed normally, *inline*. Then of course our *div* element is displayed *inline*. Unfortunately, this gives us a large white area above the other *inline* elements in order to accommodate the *div* element's larger height. It doesn't look like *display* is a good solution, either.

Let's try a different approach. Rather than changing the method in which our *div* displays, let's use the *position* rule to take it out of the content flow of the page. We can use *absolute* positioning for this, and give it an offset, as shown here:

```
#target-left{
    background-color: red;

    width: 200px;
    height: 200px;

    position: absolute;
left: 0;
}
```

We will see this in the browser:

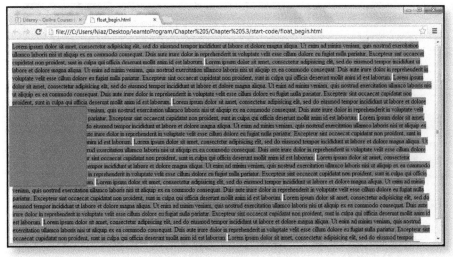

Figure 5.15: The position of the *div* element is changed after applying the *absolute* positioning rule. The text displays underneath the box.

Our *absolute* positioning rule has removed our *div* from the normal flow of the page, thus removing that awkward white space created by having such a large object in the normal flow of the line elements. What's not ideal about this solution is that these line elements have no idea that our red box *div* exists, because it has been removed from the normal flow that they are aware of. So, parts of the texts on our page are displaying underneath the red box, and that's not what we want. We'd like to see our texts wrapping or floating around the area contained by the box.

The solution lies in using the *float* rule, like so:

```
#target-left{
    background-color: red;

    width: 200px;
    height: 200px;

    float: left;
}
```

In the browser, you will see this:

Figure 5.16: The position of the *div* element after using the *float* rule. The text wraps around the box instead of continuing underneath.

Here you can see that we have succeeded in floating our *div* over a *div*-sized area that we've cut out of the display of the page. When using the *float* rule, we should keep in mind that we can only float to the left or to the right. Because of the difficulties associated with wrapping elements, we can't float an element right in the middle of a content area.

The *float* rule is an extremely powerful tool. It's easy to see how by using a left and right *div* we can do somewhat complicated things like dividing our page into two distinct left and right columns. You will also see *divs* used a lot to create a line of elements that will display one after another, no matter which elements are removed from the row, because when we float an element—in this case, to the left—it's going to go as far left as it can without hitting another floated element or the side of its content area.

Now we are going to show two *divs* lined up on the same row. In order to do this, let's create another *div* in our HTML code, like this:

```
<div id="target-left"></div><div
id="target-right"></div>
```

Here the new *div* is called 'target-right', because eventually it will be floating to the right. In our CSS, we are going to create another *id* selection rule that looks like our 'target-left' one. Let's change its background color from red to blue for the purpose of differentiating it, and float our blue *div* to the right, as shown here:

```
#target-right{
    background-color: blue;

    width: 200px;
    height: 200px;

    float: right;
}
```

We will see this in the browser:

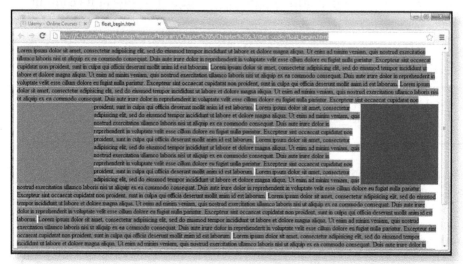

Figure 5.17: The webpage with two *div* elements. The box in the left is red, the box on the right is blue.

We can see that our text, which looks a bit different next to the two *divs* because it's aligned left, can handle changes in its display area both on the left and the right on the same line. If we *float* our blue *div* element to the left, we will see that it goes right next to the red one, in this way:

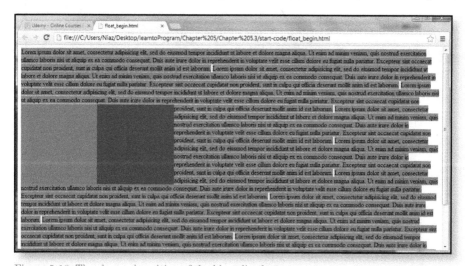

Figure 5.18: The changed position of the blue *div* element.

Here you can see that the blue *div* has moved as far left as it can, and our total display area cut-out ends up being 400 pixels wide at the left. Let's again float the blue *div* back to the right, and attempt another modification by surrounding these two *divs* with a third *div*, like this:

```
<div class="border"><div id="target-
left"></div><div id="target-right"></div></
div>
```

Let's also add the following in the CSS code:

```
.border{
    border: 5px solid black;
}
```

We should expect to see a five pixel solid border around our two *divs,*
because they are contained within an element that has this border class
attribute. In the webpage, we will see this:

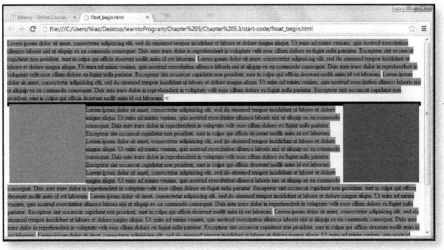

Figure 5.19: The webpage with three *div* elements. The CSS border has display issues.

Here we can see that the border displays all at once on the top, as though
it was encompassing a contained element that had no height at all, which
is of course what it's doing. By removing our two *divs* from the normal
flow of the page (the result of floating them), we've removed the ability
of our containing elements to determine how high they were. This is an
inherent weakness of floating elements. Display issues like this and our
improperly stacked *block* elements are the price we pay for removing
these elements from the normal flow of the page.

In some instances there is a solution. We can add another *div* which is assigned the class selector *.clear* as shown in the following code. This *div* has also been given an inline style that assigns a height of 20px and a background-color of green to help you see where this new *div* is positioned on the webpage, as seen in Fig 5-20.

```
<div class="border">
<div id="target-left"></div><div
id="target-right"></div> <div class="clear"
style="background-color: green; height:
20px;"></div>
</div>
<span class="clear show-bkg">Lorem ipsum
dolor sit amet, [...]
```

In the last line of this code, note that we have assigned the class selector *.clear* to the span element right after our div classes.

Now add the definition of the class style *.clear* in our CSS code:

```
.clear{
    clear: both;
}
```

The *clear* property instructs an element not to wrap around a floated item. By assigning the *.clear* style to the <div> element and the <span> element right after the <div> element with an id of *.target-right,* we are forcing those two elements to stay below the <div> element that contains our red and blue <div> areas.

In the browser, we will see this:

Figure 5.20: The border is displayed perfectly. The added *div* shows green.

The <div> element with a background color of green and a height of 20 pixels can be clearly seen.

Here we can see that the border is displayed, as expected. The price we pay for clearing our *divs* in this manner is that our content no longer wraps in between them.

If you have a firm grasp of *position, display* and *float* rules, you should be able to setup a basic webpage in just about any configuration you can think of. Surely *floats* have some weaknesses, like only being able to float elements to the left or to the right of our page. However, using non-functional HTML elements, like divs and spans, we can quickly set up scenarios where floating an element to the left of its container is essentially floating it to the center of another object.

## QUESTIONS FOR REVIEW

1. What is the default *display* option of the *span* elements?
   a. inline      c. block
   b. inline-block      d. None of the above.

2. Which of the following positions can we float an element in?
   a. top      c. center
   b. left      d. bottom

# CHAPTER 5 LAB EXERCISE

Begin with the webpage created by LabStart.html and LabStart.css. You should get this result:

Now, float some, or all, of the page's elements to create the following displays. (Hint: Number four requires the use of clear).

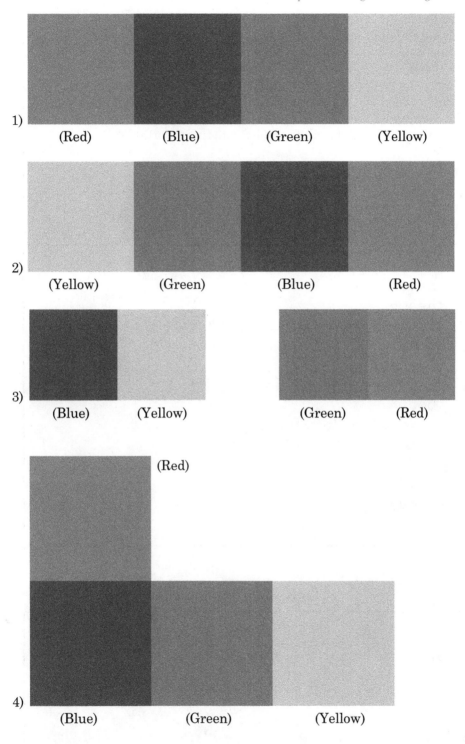

1)
(Red)    (Blue)    (Green)    (Yellow)

2)
(Yellow)    (Green)    (Blue)    (Red)

3)
(Blue)    (Yellow)    (Green)    (Red)

(Red)

4)
(Blue)    (Green)    (Yellow)

Use the display: property to create a page similar to Image 1 without relying on floats (there may be small white spaces between the <div> elements).

Modify the page so that each of the four <div> elements appears in one corner of the page. Your solution should be robust enough that resizing the browser window does not break it. What happens when the browser window is too small for all four <div>s to fit comfortably?

## Chapter 5 Lab Solutions

### Lab Solution HTML

```html
<!DOCTYPE html>
<html>
<head>
    <link rel="stylesheet" type="text/css"
href="LabSolution.css" media="screen"/>
</head>

<body>
    <div id="div1"></div>
    <div id="div2"></div>
    <div id="div3"></div>
    <div id="div4"></div>
</body>
</html>
```

### Lab Solution CSS

```css
/* Image 1
div{
    float: left;
    display: inline-block
}
*/
```

```
/* Image 2
div{
    float: right;
    display: inline-block;
}
*/

/* Image 3
div{
    display: inline-block;
}
#div1, #div3{
    float: right;
}

#div2, #div4{
    float: left;
}
*/

/*Image 4*/
div{
    display: inline-block;
    float: left;
}
#div2
{
    clear: left;
}

div{
    /*For corner position...*/
    /*position: absolute;*/
}

#div1{
    width:200px;
    height: 200px;
    background-color: red;
```

```css
    /*For corner position...*/
    top:0;
    left:0;
}

#div2{
    width:200px;
    height: 200px;
    background-color: blue;

    /*For corner position...*/
    top:0;
    right:0;
}

#div3{
    width:200px;
    height: 200px;
    background-color: green;

    /*For corner position...*/
    bottom:0;
    left:0;
}

#div4{
    width:200px;
    height: 200px;
    background-color: orange;

    /*For corner position...*/
    bottom:0;
    right:0;
}
```

# CHAPTER 5 SUMMARY

In this chapter you learned how to use the *block* and *inline* elements in order to style the webpage in an aesthetically pleasing manner. You have also gained some hands-on experience regarding the use of the *display* attribute of the elements and also the effect of using this attribute in different ways.

We have explored the available options for positioning the elements of our webpage. We have also learned how to properly use the *float* attribute in order to position the elements in a variety of ways.

In the next chapter, we will discuss the things that should be kept in mind when designing and styling the webpage to be displayed in the mobile browser.

# CSS FOR MOBILE

## CHAPTER OBJECTIVES:

- You will understand different techniques for designing mobile-friendly websites.
- You will learn where to get the tools you'll need to test your webpage on a handheld device emulator.
- You will understand how to create a webpage that will display appropriately on both large and small screen sizes.

# 6.1 TESTING WEBPAGES ON MOBILE DEVICES

The number of users who view webpages on their cell phone or tablet, rather than a traditional desktop or laptop, is increasing every year. Mobile devices employ a wide range of web browsers, some of which are very similar to traditional desktop web browsers, and others that have much smaller screen sizes. For this reason, it is very important that you test your website design on as many devices as possible before putting it online for the world to see. This can be a daunting task, and one of the main problems here is obtaining all of the devices to test on.

Fortunately, to test a new website on an Android phone, an iPhone and an iPad, we don't actually need to physically have all three of these devices. We can use an **emulator,** which is software that we can run on our desktop or laptop that will act as though it was one of these mobile devices. In this chapter, you will learn how to access a webpage that we have created through a mobile device emulator.

For the testing methodology we are going to describe here, we need to acquire two pieces of software. The first of these is the *emulator* for the device we would like to test. In this chapter, we will be viewing our webpage on an Android phone emulator. If you want to acquire this emulator, you should download the Android SDK that is freely available on the internet, which is pictured in the following screenshot:

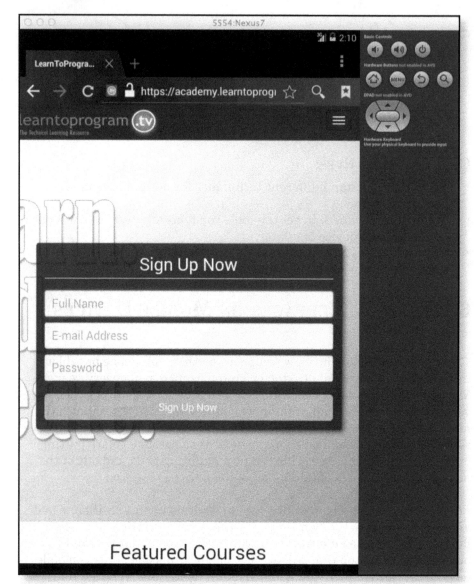

Figure 6.1: Android SDK emulator.

Installing the Android SDK requires that you have previously installed the Java SDK. If you aren't familiar with Android, you can choose to download the emulator for any mobile device that you are comfortable with. It's important to remember, however, that before putting your website online, you should always test it in a number of different emulators.

# DOWNLOADING THE MOBILE TESTING ENVIRONMENT

The mobile testing environment used in this chapter is available for free and is available for both PC and Mac operating systems. Recently, Google has made the process for installation of the Android development and testing environment much easier. Follow these steps carefully and you should have no problem testing your CSS in a mobile environment.

1) Verify that your system has the Java JDK installed. You can do this by issuing the command java –version in your command line. If your command line replies with information about the version of Java you have, you're good to go. If not you'll need to install Java.

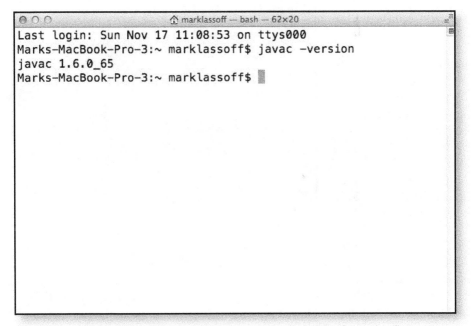

Figure 6.2: Command Line indicating that Java is installed. (Mac Operating System).

2) If you need to install the Java JDK (Java development kit) on your system, refer to http://www.oracle.com/technetwork/java/javase/downloads/index.html. There you will provide a link to download the JDK and download instructions.

3) Once you have installed or verified that the JDK is installed on your system, you can download Google's Android Development kit and tools. If you visit http://developer.android.com/sdk/index.html, the entire download and installation process is documented and a single-click install

button is available.

4) The simple Mongoose web server is available at https://code.google.com/p/mongoose/. The download and installation instructions are available on that page.

5) Once you have all three components downloaded, you will need to create and run an Android emulator. The easiest way to do this is to run Eclipse from the Android Development kit you downloaded from developer.android.com. Inside the folder you downloaded is an Eclipse folder. Navigate to that folder and double-click the Eclipse icon.

6) When Eclipse opens it will ask you to confirm the default workspace. Click through that dialog box and you'll be in the Eclipse environment. You'll see an icon in the upper left of the Eclipse environment that looks like a small smart phone—that's the Android Device manager, or AVD for short.

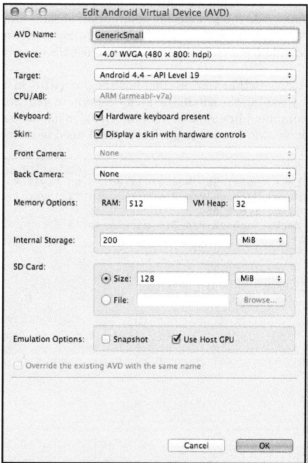

Figure 6.3: Configuring the Android Virtual Device in the device manager.

7) Click the AVD. When it loads, click the new button. Configure your device according to the screenshot 6.3.

8) Click *Okay*. Make sure your device is selected in the Android Virtual Device Manager window and click *Start*.

9) It will likely take several minutes (depending on resources available on your system) for your virtual device to start. You may now test according to the instructions in this chapter.

The second piece of software we are going to need is a web server. Because emulators simulate entirely new devices, they don't actually have easy access to the file system on your computer where your HTML and CSS files are located. The easiest way to give your device access to these files is to place them on your local network. That's where the web server comes in. For this chapter we will be using the Mongoose web server, because it's extremely simple to use. To acquire this web server, download and run the .exe file from this site: https://code.google.com/p/mongoose/. (There is also a Mac version of Mongoose available at https://code.google.com/p/mongoose-mac-package/.)

The great thing about the Mongoose project is that it can be used in a variety of platforms. So, even if you are working in Linux or Unix instead of Windows, you should not face any problems.

Once you have downloaded the Mongoose executable file, you should place it in the same folder where your HTML and CSS files are located. That's because we are not going to be modifying any of the Mongoose server's settings, we are simply going to be running it using its defaults.

If we simply run the executable file, it's going to serve up the folder that it's located in. To make sure that our web server is working properly, let's use our desktop web browser to quickly navigate to that directory. To do this, we need to give our web browser two pieces of information. First, it needs the IP address of the local machine, and we can always get that by simply using the *localhost* keyword. We follow that with a colon (:), and then we need to tell it what port we would like it to request on. In this case, we are going to use port 8080, so the entire address is localhost:8080. If everything is set up correctly, the result should be similar to this screenshot:

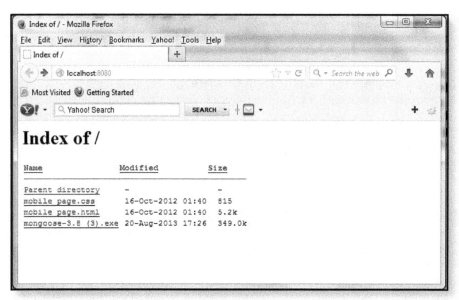

Figure 6.4: The webpage showing the local directory.

Here, we can see the contents of the directory where we launched the mongoose.exe file. We can also see the mobile_page.html file, which is the website we want our emulator to be able to view. This website will look like this in our web browser:

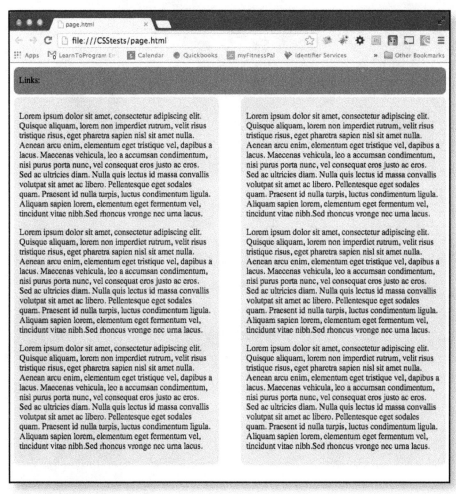

Figure 6.5: The webpage that will be viewed in the emulator later on.

Now, let's go back to our device emulator. We can't navigate our emulator to the *localhost* in the way that we did from our desktop. That's because *localhost* will navigate to this device itself, which believes itself to be completely separate from the web browser window that it's running in. Instead, we can use the IP address 10.0.2.2 to access the machine this emulator is running on. From there, we can once again navigate to the port 8080, in this way: 10.0.2.2:8080. Port 8080 is the default port for a debug- or development-level server. If we submit this IP address, we will get our file system index back, where we will find our HTML file called mobile_page.html.

If we open it, we will see the following:

Figure 6.6: Our webpage is opened in the Android emulator.

This is what our webpage will look like on an Android device. This is the most efficient way to view websites on many mobile devices. It's also the first step towards developing mobile-friendly websites.

## QUESTIONS FOR REVIEW

1. What is an emulator?
   a. Hardware.
   b. Software.
   c. A method.
   d. None of the above

2. Which is the default port for a debug- or development-level server?
   a. 8060
   b. 8070
   c. 8080
   d. 8090

# 6.2 ELEGANT CSS FOR THE MOBILE WORLD

In this section we will take a look at how we can use different CSS rules to display our webpages with more clarity on mobile devices. We will be modifying the following webpage so that it becomes more mobile device friendly.

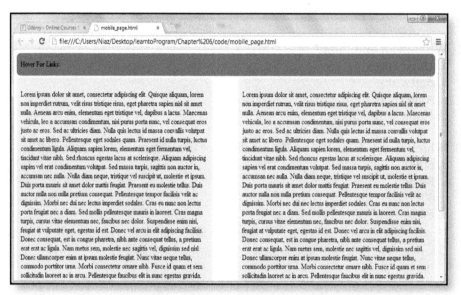

Figure 6.7: The webpage that we will be modifying.

This webpage has two columns, which are contained by *div* elements floated left and right. There is also a header at the top of the page, which will display some links when we hover over it, as shown here:

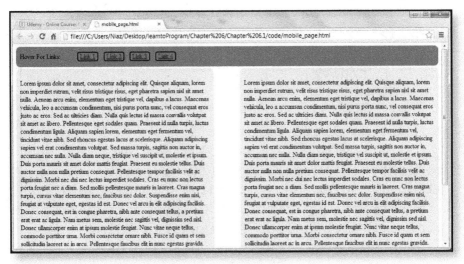

Figure 6.8: The webpage with links.

Let's examine the corresponding HTML code:

## CODE LISTING: PRE-MOBILE FRIENDLY HTML

```
<!DOCTYPE html>
<html>
<head>
    <link rel="stylesheet" type="text/css"
href="normal_page.css" media="Screen"/>
</head>

<body>
    <div id="header">
        <div class="header-show-
always">Links:</div>
        <div class="header-show-hover">
            <ul class="horizontal-list">
            <li><a href="badlink">Link 1</
a></li>
            <li><a href="badlink">Link 2</
a></li>
            <li><a href="badlink">Link 3</
a></li>
```

```
                <li><a href="badlink">Link 4</
a></li>
            </ul>
        </div>
    </div>

    <div id="left-column">
        <p>Lorem ipsum dolor sit amet,
consectetur adipiscing elit. Quisque
aliquam, lorem non imperdiet rutrum, velit
risus tristique risus, eget pharetra sapien
nisl sit amet nulla. Aenean arcu enim,
elementum eget tristique vel, dapibus a
lacus. Maecenas vehicula, leo a accumsan
condimentum, nisi purus porta nunc, vel
consequat eros justo ac eros. Sed ac
ultricies diam. Nulla quis lectus id massa
convallis volutpat sit amet ac libero.
Pellentesque eget sodales quam. Praesent id
nulla turpis, luctus condimentum ligula.
Aliquam sapien lorem, elementum eget
fermentum vel, tincidunt vitae nibh.Sed
rhoncus ………… nec urna lacus.
        </p>
    </div>

    <div id="right-column">
        <p>Lorem ipsum dolor sit amet,
consectetur adipiscing elit. Quisque
aliquam, lorem non imperdiet rutrum, velit
risus tristique risus, eget pharetra sapien
nisl sit amet nulla. Aenean arcu enim,
elementum eget tristique vel, dapibus a
lacus. Maecenas vehicula, leo a accumsan
condimentum, nisi purus porta nunc, vel
consequat eros justo ac eros. Sed ac
ultricies diam. Nulla quis lectus id massa
convallis volutpat sit amet ac libero.
```

```
Pellentesque eget sodales quam. Praesent id
nulla turpis, luctus condimentum ligula.
Aliquam sapien lorem, elementum eget
fermentum vel, tincidunt vitae nibh.Sed
rhoncus ………… nec urna lacus.

        </p>
    </div>
</body>
</html>
```

And the CSS code:

### CODE LISTING: PRE-MOBILE FRIENDLY CSS

```css
#header{
    height: 25px;

    background-color: green;
    padding-top: 5px;
    border: 10px green solid;
    border-radius: 10px;
    margin-bottom: 5px;
}
    #header .header-show-always{
        display: inline;
    }
    #header .header-show-hover{
        display:none;
    }
    #header:hover .header-show-hover{
        display: inline;
    }

#left-column{
    float: left;
    width: 45%;
```

```css
        background-color: rgb(230,230,200);
        border: 10px rgb(230,230,200) solid;
        border-radius: 10px;
}

#right-column{
        float: right;
        width: 45%;

        background-color: rgb(230,230,200);
        border: 10px rgb(230,230,200) solid;
        border-radius: 10px;
}

.horizontal-list{
        display:inline;
}

.horizontal-list li{
        display: inline;

        border: 2px solid black;
        border-radius: 5px;
        padding-left: 5px;
        padding-right: 5px;
        margin-right: 10px;
}
```

Using the technique previously described, let's see how this webpage looks on a mobile device, in this case, an Android phone:

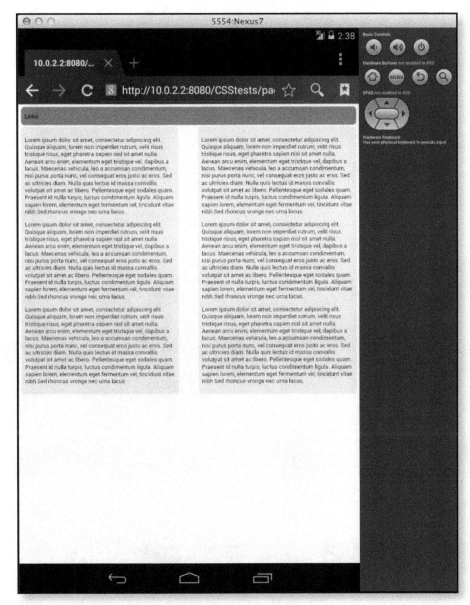

Figure 6.9: The view of the webpage on an Android phone emulator.

We can see that on an Android phone emulator, this page is not very clear. We can identify three major issues with it. First, the text on this webpage appears very small on the screen—much too small to be readable. We can use the zoom controls to magnify the screen so it appears something like this:

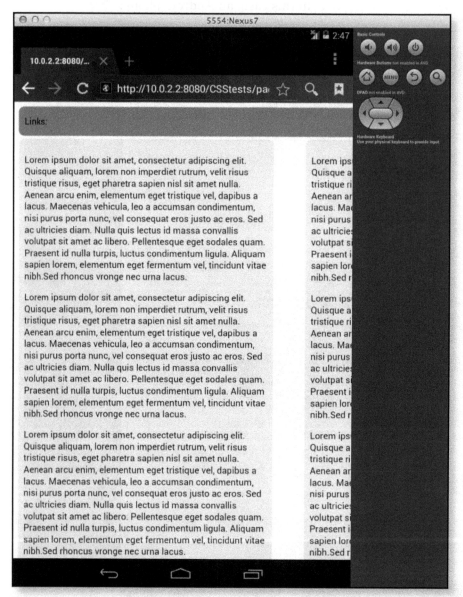

Figure 6.10: The page is zoomed-in on the emulator.

The second issue is the view of the left and right floated columns. Once we've zoomed-in this page to a readable degree, the user has no way of knowing that there is something for them to view to the left or to the right. Mobile webpages are expected to order content vertically, rather than horizontally.

Lastly, our default webpage expected users to mouse over the 'Links' section to see the links. This is really a frustrating matter when the page appears on a mobile device, because most of these devices use a touch screen. In order to see these links, a user would have to press their finger on the green box. That finger would likely obscure the links themselves, or worse, unintentionally select one.

Let's again look at the webpage on the emulator from a slightly altered perspective:

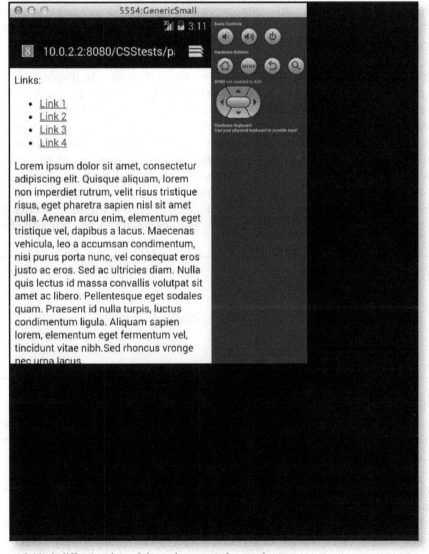

Figure 6.11: A different view of the webpage on the emulator.

Here, we can see that the text in the text box does not fill the entire available area of the screen, which looks awkward. First, the mobile web browser, which renders the content, is applying some rules from the default style sheet. Mobile web browsers will generally restrict the width of the text elements so that users can see them at a reasonably zoomed-in view. Users don't like to scroll left and right while viewing a webpage on mobile devices.

The second reason why the text element does not encompass the entire box is because we fixed the width of the box using a percentage of the maximum page width. This demonstrates that mobile web development is set up under the assumption that you are not going to apply fixed widths to your elements.

Although our main goal while designing the webpage is to display it perfectly on the web browser of a desktop or laptop computer, it is also necessary to modify this page so that it displays in a more mobile-friendly manner. There are two options for us here. One, we can simply remove the CSS styling from this page when viewed on mobile devices. Although this sounds more radical, in a lot of cases where we don't want to expend the effort to create a brand-new CSS sheet for mobile devices, it's a very good solution. The other option available is to create a different set of CSS rules for our mobile devices. To do this, we are going to be working in the head of the HTML code. In our case, we have the following in the HTML head element:

```
<head>
    <link rel="stylesheet" type="text/
css" href="normal_page_begin.css"
media="Screen"/>
</head>
```

When we link a stylesheet in HTML, one of the media attributes is used to determine the type of media the stylesheet should be applied to. Most often we associate the "screen" value with the media attribute, meaning that the CSS is intended for the screen as opposed to print.

You can also associate the "handheld" value with the media attribute which will apply the stylesheet to handheld devices. However, this is not a contemporary solution. As mobile devices and their web browsers are becoming more and more powerful, most of these devices no longer register themselves as 'handheld' devices, because their local web browsers and their resolution is high enough that they can display high-end CSS effects. That does not mean, however, that we never want to target them with separate CSS, as we just saw, some pages just don't look good on the screen-size of the mobile device. If they haven't registered themselves as handheld, we can target them by taking a look at the width of their screen. If they have a resolution below a certain width, we can declare them to be handheld devices, or small-screen, and write our separate CSS for them. In order to do this, we are going to need to do two things in our HTML. First, we have to declare a meta tag, and modify the code in this way:

```
<head>
    <meta name="viewport"
content="width=device-width"/>
    <link rel="stylesheet" type="text/css"
href="normal_page.css" media="Screen and
(min-device-width:481px)"/>

</head>
```

In order to ensure mobile devices do not implement this stylesheet, we have made the *media* rule more restrictive. Let's say that in addition to the device having a screen, it must also have a certain *device-width*. Here, we need to choose a value of the *device-width* that is large enough for our device to display appropriately. A width that is often used is 480 pixels, as a threshold between a small device and a medium-sized one. If 480 pixels is for a small device, then our minimum *device-width* for having our stylized display is going to be 481 pixels. If we take a look at our mobile device, we will see this:

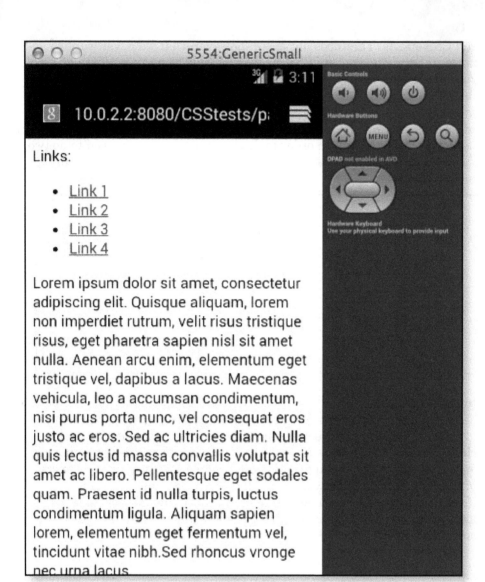

Figure 6.12: The changed style of the webpage, which is now more mobile-friendly.

The CSS styling on our page is removed now, because the device-width here is not large enough to display the styling properties of CSS. It can be argued that this is a superior webpage from the mobile point of view than the previous page. It's certainly not as pretty, but it is much more functional for the user. The links are easily accessible, and the user only needs to scroll vertically to read all of the text on the page. However, we can see from our desktop web browser that our old styling still applies, because this device conforms to our *min-device-width* rule that we just applied, and its width is definitely more than 480 pixels in this case.

Now, let's say that we want the website on our mobile device to still look thematically similar to the larger version. In order to do this, we are going to write separate CSS rules for our mobile site. So, we are going to need a new HTML *stylesheet* rule, which is shown here:

```
<head>
    <meta name="viewport"
content="width=device-width"/>

<link rel="stylesheet" type="text/css"
href="normal_page.css" media="Screen and
(min-device-width:481px)"/>

<link rel="stylesheet" type="text/css"
href="mobile_page.css" media="Screen and
(max-device-width:480px)"/>


</head>
```

Here, we have created a new stylesheet that we are calling "mobile_page. css", and saved it in the same directory. We have also modified the *media* rule so that it applies to the mobile devices, where the maximum device-width is 480 pixels.

Let's work on our new CSS file which has been created for smaller devices. We should add the following CSS code in this file:

```
@media (max-device-width:480px){

    #header{
        background-color: red;
    }

}
```

In our mobile device emulator, we will see this:

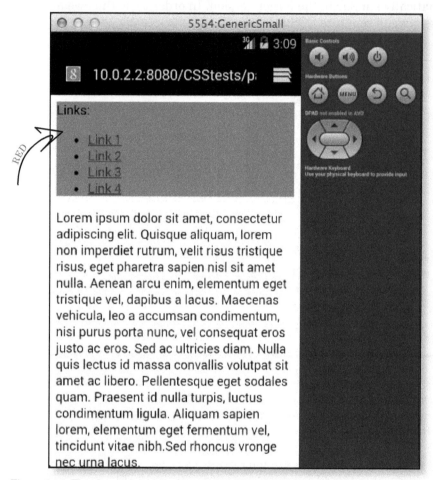

Figure 6.13: The changed design of our webpage on the mobile device emulator.

Here we see that the links, which are the header elements of the page, now have a red background.

Generally, when we're setting up a web software project and we know that we are going to support both desktop browsers and small-device browsers, we're going to write three CSS pages. In addition to our present CSS files called normal_page.css and mobile_page.css, we're going to have a basic page, which we call base_page.css. This is the stylesheet that we'd like to apply for all types of browsers; in this case, elements like the background color of our elements, so that our webpage has a style that works across all of the other size-specific pages that we write.

Let's modify the HTML head in this way:

```
<head>
    <meta name="viewport"
content="width=device-width"/>
    <link rel="stylesheet" type="text/css"
href="base_page.css" media="Screen"/>
    <link rel="stylesheet" type="text/css"
href="normal_page.css" media="(min-device-
width:481px)"/>
    <link rel="stylesheet" type="text/css"
href="mobile_page.css" media="(max-device-
width:480px)"/>
</head>
```

In the CSS file called base_page.css, let's add the following code:

```
#header{
    background-color: green;
    padding-top: 5px;
    border: 10px green solid;
    border-radius: 10px;
    margin-bottom: 5px;
}

#left-column{
    background-color: rgb(230,230,200);
    border: 10px rgb(230,230,200) solid;
    border-radius: 10px;
}

#right-column{
    background-color: rgb(230,230,200);
    border: 10px rgb(230,230,200) solid;
    border-radius: 10px;
}
```

```
.horizontal-list li{
    padding-left: 5px;
    padding-right: 5px;
    margin-right: 10px;
}
```

I mentioned earlier that the general rule for mobile development is that you should never explicitly set the widths of the elements, because these limit the mobile browser's ability to accurately display the elements. So, if we compare this code with that of our normal_page.css, we can see that we have eliminated the *width* rules in this CSS code for the basic page. Moreover, in order to ensure that the users can view our page in its entirety simply by scrolling up and down, we have removed the floating of the elements and this will result in the columns stacking on top of each other.

Another thing we should keep in mind is that the *border-radius* is a CSS3 property, so it might not yet be supported by all major mobile web browsers. There are certainly some less common mobile browsers that aren't supporting *border-radius*. It is permissible to leave the *border-radius* code in the CSS, however, since it will simply be ignored by browsers that don't implement it. The border-radius has no effect on the readability of our site, just the aesthetics.

On our list, let's just eliminate the borders for our list items, because those will likely distract the user. In order to make sure that our lists are displayed vertically, we have removed the *inline* display property of the list items. If we test the page in the web browser, we will see this:

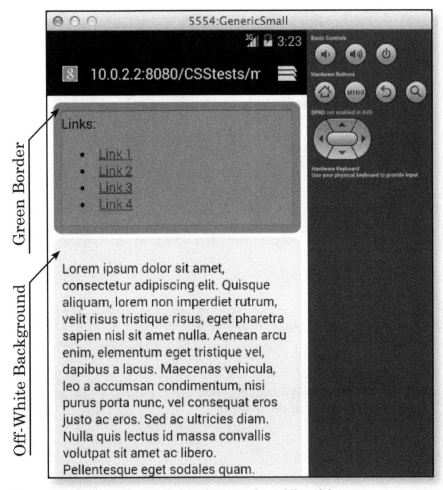

Figure 6.14: The altered view of our webpage at the mobile web browser.

This is a very mobile-friendly webpage, and it retains a lot of the visual styling that the larger version of our page had. This means that the users will have similar experiences while browsing the webpage in both a desktop and a mobile device.

In a recent survey, it was identified that mobile devices made up more than 20% of our web traffic. Hence, professional web developers around the world are putting high emphasis on designing mobile-friendly websites.

QUESTIONS FOR REVIEW

1. Which width is often used as a threshold between a small device and a medium-sized one?
   a. 460 pixels.
   b. 470 pixels.
   c. 480 pixels.
   d. 490 pixels.

2. According to the general rule for mobile development, what should you never explicitly set?
   a. The width of the element.
   b. The height of the element.
   c. The weight of the element.
   d. The background color of the element.

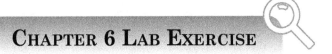

# CHAPTER 6 LAB EXERCISE

Set up an emulator for a mobile device with a small screen. Side by side with your desktop web browser, visit some websites you commonly use. Make note of how the pages display differently on the desktop and mobile browsers. Which pages adapt well to the mobile environment? Which do not? Can you tell when mobile-specific CSS is being applied?

Create a CSS and HTML webpage that appears blank to most users. Leave a secret message for users on mobile devices though!

Add a *div* to your HTML page and place a lot of text in it. Style this *div* to have a width greater than your mobile device's resolution and give the *div* a background so that you can see the area it encompasses. View this *div* on your mobile emulator and a desktop web browser. How do the two web browsers display the text differently? If you increase the width of the *div* to be wider than the resolution of your desktop browser, does this browser react in the same manner that the mobile one did?

```html
<!DOCTYPE html>
<html>
<head>
    <meta name="viewport"
content="width=device-width"/>
    <link rel="stylesheet" type="text/css"
href="LabSolution.css" media="Screen and
(max-device-width:480px)"/>
    <style type="text/css">
        .hidden{
            visibility: hidden;
        }
    }
    </style>
</head>

<body>
    <div class="hidden">
        <p>This Text Will Only Show To
Mobile Users This Text Will Only Show To
Mobile Users This Text Will Only Show To
Mobile Users This Text Will Only Show To
Mobile Users This Text Will Only Show To
Mobile Users This Text Will Only Show To
Mobile Users This Text Will Only Show To
Mobile Users This Text Will Only Show To
Mobile Users This Text Will Only Show To
Mobile Users ............... This Text Will Only
Show To Mobile Users
        </p>
    </div>
</body>
</html>
```

## LAB SOLUTIONS CSS

```
@media (max-device-width:480px){
    .hidden{
        visibility: visible !important;

        width: 500px;
        background-color: grey;
    }
}
```

# CHAPTER 6 SUMMARY

As the trend of browsing websites through mobile devices has been increasing rapidly around the world, a significant amount of research is going on to make the webpages more mobile-friendly. In this chapter, we have learned what to do when designing and styling our webpages for mobile devices. We have understood what tools are required and where to find them to test our webpages in a mobile device emulator.

We have also learned in this chapter what we'll need to set up our webpage so that it will keep the same overall look and feel while adapting to the size of the screen that the user is viewing it on.

# ANSWER KEY: CSS DEVELOPMENT (WITH CSS3!)

## Chapter 1.5 Introducing CSS3

1. Which web development technology can be used to make a website more visually appealing?
Answer: b. CSS

2. Which of the following is correctly defined as a valid rgb style?
Answer: c. rgb(255,0,255)

3. Which of the following is not a proper way to deploy CSS on a HTML page?
Answer: c. In-child

4. Which is the latest version of CSS as approved by W3C?
Answer: b. CSS3

## Chapter 2.1 Styling Text Elements

1. The property to effectively handle the presence of spaces, tabs and new lines is called what?
Answer: a. White-space property

2. Which rule is used to make sure that when we put our mouse over the menu, something will be displayed?
Answer: b. hover

## Chapter 2.2 Styling Tables and Lists

1. What option do we use to remove the double border around each cell of a table to ensure that there is a single border?
Answer: b. border-collapse

2. Which of the following is the correct way to insert a picture as the bullet of the lists?
Answer: a. list-style-image: url("picture.png");

## Chapter 2.3 Styling Backgrounds

1. Which of the following styles in CSS is used to display an image in the background?
Answer: a. background-image

2. Which of the following allows us to declare multiple background images for a single element?
Answer: c. CSS3

## Chapter 2.4 The Sliding-Door Technique (Making a CSS Button)

1. Which rule takes two or more images and attempts to display them so that they appear to be one image of any size?
Answer: a. sliding door technique.

2. How can you ensure that the button is only resized horizontally?
Answer: a. By giving it a mandatory height.

## Chapter 2.5 Sprite Sheets and Images

1. What are individual images in a sprite sheet called?
Answer: c. Sprites.

2. Which of the following is not an advantage of using sprite sheets?
Answer: a. Sprite sheets look more attractive.

## 2.6 Creating a Drop-Down Menu with CSS

1. What rule can you use to increase the space between the tags in a menu?
Answer: a. Padding.

2. Which of the following rules is used to remove bullets from the lists?
Answer: a. list-style-type: none

## Chapter 3.1 Introduction to the Box Model

1. How many layers are there in a box model?
Answer: c. Five.

2. Which of the following is not a layer in the box model?
Answer:  d. Display Layer.

## Chapter 3.2 The Content Area

1. Which property allows us to explicitly define how an element handles the content area which is too small for it?
Answer: a. Overflow.

2. Which of the following is not a possible value for the *overflow* attribute?
Answer: d. Invisible.

## Chapter 3.3 Border and Outline Styling

1. Which of the following options can we use to ensure that the border won't be displayed at all?
Answer: b. hidden.

2. Which of the following options is used to give our border a three-dimensional look?
Answer: a. inset.

## Chapter 3.4 Working with Margins and Padding

1. Which rule defines that the elements separated by margins are separated by less distance than the elements separated by padding?
Answer: a. margin-collapse

## Chapter 4.1 CSS3 Transforms

1. Which action can't you perform by using the CSS transform rule?
Answer: d. animate

2. Which of the following options is used to move an image element?
Answer: a. translate

## Chapter 4.2 CSS3 Transitions

1. Which web browser can CSS3 transforms not be used in?
Answer: b. Internet Explorer.

2. How many attributes do CSS transitions have?
Answer: b. Two.

## Chapter 4.3 CSS3 Animations

1. CSS3 animations cannot be used in which web browser?
Answer: a. Internet Explorer.

2. The code to define all of the keyframes is prefaced with which symbol?
Answer: b. @

## Chapter 5.1 The Display Property

1. Which type of elements force new lines at their beginning and end?
Answer: a. block

2. Which *display* property is used when we want the *block* elements to ignore the forcing of new lines at their beginning and end?
Answer: c. inline-block

## Chapter 5.2 In-Depth CSS Positioning

1. How many offset rules are there?
Answer: d. Five.

2. What is the default position of the span elements of our page?
Answer: a. static

## Chapter 5.3 Floating Elements

1. What is the default *display* option of the *span* elements?
Answer: a. inline

2. Which of the following positions can we float element in?
Answer: b. left

## Chapter 6.1 Testing Webpages on Mobile Devices

1. What is an emulator?
Answer: b. Software.

2. Which is the default port for a debug- or development-level server?
Answer: c. 8080

## Chapter 6.2 Elegant CSS for the Mobile World

1. Which width is often used as a threshold between a small device and a medium-sized one?
Answer: c. 480 pixels

2. According to the general rule for mobile development, what should you never explicitly set?
 Answer: a. The width of the element.

*CSS Development (with CSS3!)*

# Appendix: CSS Rules or Terms

| CSS Rules/ Terms | Definitions/Descriptions |
|---|---|
| @font-face | This directive (used in the format @font-face) informs a browser of the name of a new font and provides the URL to where the browser can download the font. |
| @keyframes | This is a CSS3 at rule (not a CSS property) that defines the keyframes to be used in an animation. A name is assigned to the defined keyframes. This name is then applied to the element to be animated. |
| absolute positioning | Absolute positioning of an element lets you place it on a webpage by specifying its left, right, top, or bottom position using units of pixels, ems or percentages. Absolute is one of the values of the position property. Absolutely positioned elements are ignored in the normal flow of the page. |
| ancestor | A selector or tag is known as the ancestor of those selectors or tags which are contained within it. (See descendant.) |
| animation | CSS3 animation is the process of moving from one set of properties (defined in a keyframe) to another set (defined in another keyframe) to another set and so on. (In CSS3 transitions you only move between two sets of properties and no keyframes are required for transitions.) |
| Android | This is an open source, Linux-based operating system created and maintained by a group of software and hardware companies and operators called the Open Handset Alliance. |
| animation property | This property provides a compact way of including the following seven animation properties into one style rule: animation-name, animation-duration, animation-timing-function, animation-iteration-count, animation-direction, animation-delay, and animation-fill-mode. |

| CSS Rules/ Terms | Definitions/Descriptions |
| --- | --- |
| animation-delay | This animation property instructs the browser to delay executing an animation by a specified number of seconds or milliseconds. |
| animation-direction | This animation property specifies the starting point for animations that execute more than once. By setting this property to the value alternate, the animation's first run will be from its starting properties to its ending properties and then its second run will be from its ending properties to its starting properties and then its third run will be from start to end and so on. The default value is the standard setting of normal. |
| animation-duration | This animation property specifies in seconds or milliseconds how long it will take for an animation to complete. |
| animation-fill-mode | This animation property determines how an element will be styled at the start and/or finish of an animation. Valid values are backwards, forwards, or both. Forwards leaves the element styled as at the end of the animation instead of displaying the element as it looked before the animation started. |
| animation-iteration-count | This animation property instructs the browser how many times to run the animation. This property can be assigned an integer value or infinite to indicate non-stop execution of the animation. |
| animation-name | This property is used to assign a name to the keyframes that have been created with the @ keyframes at rule. This name is then assigned to the HTML element to be animated. |
| animation-timing-function | This animation property sets the speed of an animation as it executes within the specified animation duration. |

| CSS Rules/ Terms | Definitions/Descriptions |
|---|---|
| background | This is the lowest layer of an HTML element. The background can be set to either a color or an image and it lies beneath the content, padding and border areas of the box model. |
| background-image | This property specifies the image that will be used as the background. This property's value is the path to the image specified without quotation marks. Example: url(images/background.png). |
| background-position | This property specifies the initial position of a background image, if an image is specified. |
| background-repeat | This property specifies how an image tiles or repeats itself. It accepts four values: repeat, no-repeat, repeat-x and repeat-y. |
| background-size | This property is used to scale up, scale down or even distort the dimensions and proportions of background images. It can be set to specific values of pixels, ems, or percentages or to the values contain or cover. If set to contain, the image will be resized to fit the element while maintaining its aspect ratio. If set to cover, the width and height of the image will be forced to fit the width and height of the element which in most cases results in some distortion of the image. |
| block | This value for the display property forces a line break before and after the element. The element will be displayed just like a paragraph and a header, which are block elements. |
| border | In the box model, this is the area between the padding and the margin. It can never be set to a negative value or a percentage. The background extends into the border area. |

| CSS Rules/ Terms | Definitions/Descriptions |
|---|---|
| border-collapse | This property works only when applied to a <table> tag. When it is set to the value of separate, borders around a table's cells are separated from each other by a few pixels of space. This results in double borders between the table's cells. When this property is set to the value of collapse, the space between borders is removed and only one border appears between a table's cells. |
| border-image | Using the border-image property, we can take an image file and turn it into a border that we can place around any element. |
| border-radius | This property creates rectangular borders with rounded corners. This works only if the element has a border, background color or image. |
| box model | The CSS Box Model describes the rectangular boxes that are generated for every HTML element on a web page. Each box has a content area (e.g. text, image, etc.), surrounded by a padding area, then a border area and finally a margin area. |
| browser (web browser) | A computer program with a graphical user interface for retrieving, presenting and searching information resources, usually stored in HTML format, on the World Wide Web. |
| color | This property is used to set the foreground color of an element's text content. |
| cascading property of CSS | CSS gives preference to the rules that are more specific or to the most recently declared rule. |
| child | This is the tag or selector that is the closest descendant of another tag or selector. It is the tag that is in the immediate level below the parent tag. |

| CSS Rules/ Terms | Definitions/Descriptions |
| --- | --- |
| class selector | A class selector applies style rules to elements that have the equivalent class attribute in their opening HTML tag. The selector is created by prefixing the class name with a period. (For example, the class selector .classname applies to all elements that have the class="classname" attribute.) |
| clear | This property instructs an element not to wrap around a floated item. This forces the element to stay below the floated item. |
| CSS | Cascading Style Sheets, abbreviated as CSS, is a web development language that allows you to determine the visual appearance of HTML pages in popular web browsers. |
| CSS3 | The latest version of CSS approved by the W3C (World Wide Web Consortium). |
| CSS3 Vendor Prefix | A unique prefix that identifies each browser. These prefixes allow browsers to experimentally and innovatively implement a proposed W3C standard. The prefixes of the more popular browsers are: -moz- (Firefox), -o- (Opera), -webkit- (Safari, Chrome, Konqueror), -ms- (Internet Explorer 9+) |
| child selector (>) | A child selector (denoted by a right angle bracket ">") instructs the browser to apply style rules to a specific child of a specific parent. For example, li > p selects any <p> tag that is a child of a <li> tag. |
| descendant | A selector or tag is called the descendant of another selector or tag if it is contained within the latter at any level. See "ancestor". |
| display | This property instructs the browser how to display an HTML element. The commonly used values for this property are: block, inline-block, inline, list-item, none. |

| CSS Rules/ Terms | Definitions/Descriptions |
|---|---|
| emulator | Software that runs on a desktop computer that mimics accurately the features, behavior and capabilities of a mobile device. An emulator allows developers of software for mobile devices to test their software on the emulator instead of on different mobile devices. |
| fixed positioning | HTML elements with fixed positioning are locked into their place on the screen even as the web page is scrolled up or down by the user. |
| float | This property determines whether an HTML block-level element floats to the left, right or not at all. It applies only to elements that are not absolutely positioned. Values are: left, right, none. The value none turns off floating entirely. |
| font-family | This property declares the name of the font to be used to display the text of an element. |
| hover | This pseudo-class selector (used in the format :hover and placed right after a tag selector, e.g. a:hover) provides instructions to the browser about what actions to take when the mouse is positioned over an HTML element. |
| id selector | An id selector applies styles to elements that have the equivalent id attribute in their opening HTML tag. The selector is created by prefixing the id with the hash or pound sign (#). (For example, the id selector #idname applies to all elements that have the id="classname" attribute. |
| inline | This value for the display property will make the element display on the same line as other inline elements. Examples of inline elements are <a>, <span>, <b>, <i> and others. |
| inline-block | This value for the display property causes a block-level element to display as an inline element. |

| CSS Rules/ Terms | Definitions/Descriptions |
|---|---|
| iOS | The mobile operating system (previously iPhone OS) developed and distributed by Apple Inc. and installed in Apple's iPhone, iPad and iPod mobile devices. |
| iPhone | A line of smartphones that run iOS and are designed, developed and marketed by Apple Inc. |
| iPad | A line of tablet computers that run iOS and are designed, developed and marketed by Apple Inc. |
| keyframe | This is used in animations and defines a stage in animations where properties change. It is a single frame of animation that dictates how a scene looks. Multiple keyframes can be defined for one animation (using the at rule @keyframes) thus allowing for complex animation effects. |
| line-height | Increases or decreases the space between lines of text in a paragraph. The normal line height is 120 percent of the size of the text. |
| list-style | This property is used as a shorthand notation for list-style-image, list-style-position and list-style-type. The values of one or more of those properties are separated by spaces. |
| list-style-image | This sets the image to be used for a bullet in a bulleted list. This property's value is the path to the image specified without quotation marks. For example: url(images/bullet.png). |
| list-style-position | This property controls the position of the markers (the bullets or numbers) in a bulleted list. When set to the value of outside, the markers appear outside of the rectangle created by the text of the list item. This is the normal way that browsers display bullets. The value of inside places the markers within the rectangle created by the text of the list item. |

| CSS Rules/ Terms | Definitions/Descriptions |
|---|---|
| list-style-type | This property allows three types of bullets for unordered lists, <ul>: disc, circle, or square, and six types of numbering schemes for numbered lists, <ol>: decimal, decimal-leading-zero, upper-alpha, lower-alpha, upper-roman, lower-roman. |
| margin | In the box model, this is the area outside the border. It can be set to a negative value. Horizontally adjacent margins do not overlap. Vertically adjacent margins are collapsed. The background does not extend into the margin area. |
| margin-collapse | This rule determines how far above or below images are from each other. |
| mobile device | A gadget that is portable, personal, easy and fast to use and has some kind of network connection. Smartphones and tablets are considered mobile devices but netbooks and laptops are not. |
| mongoose (web server) | A small, easy-to-use, self-contained cross-platform web server. It does not require any external software to run. Its purpose is to provide a simple, functional, embeddable web server to provide a simple web development environment for application and device developers to test the web interfaces of their applications and device. |
| none | A value for many style properties. For the display property, this value makes the element completely disappear from the page. For the float property it turns off any floating for the element and positions it like a normal, unfloated element. |
| nowrap | This is a value for the white-space property and indicates that that no wrapping will occur. |
| outline | An outline is just like a border except that an outline takes up no space (it doesn't affect the width and height of an element). It is a rarely used component of the box model but it is used to draw attention to a portion of a webpage. |

| CSS Rules/ Terms | Definitions/Descriptions |
|---|---|
| overflow | This property controls how a browser handles content that cannot fit the dimensions of its content area. Its four values are: visible, scroll, auto and hidden. |
| parent | The tag or selector that is the closest ancestor of another tag (the child). It is the tag that is in the immediate level above the child tag. |
| padding | In the box model, this style property defines the area between the content area and the border of the CSS box model. The background extends into the padding area and padding can never be negative. |
| perspective | This property allows changing the perspective on how 3D elements are viewed. |
| position | This property instructs the browser how and where to display an element. Values for this property are: static, relative, absolute and fixed. Static is the default value so there is no need to declare it. |
| pre-wrap | This is one of the values of the white-space property and is used when we want wrapping to occur. |
| pseudo-class | A pseudo-class targets or identifies elements of a webpage that cannot be pinpointed specifically by a tag or selector or by the element's name, attributes or contents but are nonetheless easy to target or identify such as a link as you move your mouse over it. Pseudo-classes are preceded by a colon (:) and then appended to a selector or tag. Examples are :hover, :visited, :first-child, :nth-child, etc. |
| pseudo-element | Pseudo-elements are used to target or identify sub-parts of elements. They have the same format as pseudo-classes. They cannot be applied to inline styles and only one pseudo-element may be declared per selector. Some examples are :first-letter, :first-line, end :before. |

| CSS Rules/ Terms | Definitions/Descriptions |
|---|---|
| relative positioning | In relative positioning, an HTML element is placed relative to its current position in the HTML flow and the other HTML elements adjust themselves to the original position of a relatively moved element. Moving an element by relative positioning creates a hole where the element was originally placed. |
| rgb() | This is a color method which is provided as one of the values to various color properties. This method requires three parameters each representing the red, green and blue hues, respectively. |
| rotate() | A function provided as a value to the transform property which instructs the browser to rotate an element a specified number of degrees around a circle. |
| scale() | A function provided as a value to the transform property which instructs the browser to make an element larger or smaller by the value (a scaling factor) provided to the function. The horizontal and vertical dimensions of the element can be scaled separately by providing two numbers separated by a comma inside the parentheses. For example (.5, 2). The first number is the horizontal scale (which in this example is shortened by 50%) and the second number is the vertical scale whose length is doubled. |
| scaleX(), scaleY() | These two functions are provided as values to the transform property allow you to resize an html element. ScaleX() scales along the horizontal axis while scaleY() scales vertically. |
| scaleX(-1) | This will flip the element on its horizontal axis (the right side becomes the left side and vice versa.) |
| scaleY(-1) | This will flip the element on its vertical axis (making it upside down). |

| CSS Rules/ Terms | Definitions/Descriptions |
|---|---|
| scale(-1,-1) | This will combine the effects of scaleX(-1) and scaleY(-1). The element will be flipped on both horizontal and vertical axes. |
| sdk | This is an abbreviation for "software development kit". An SDK is a collection of software used for developing applications for a specific device or operating system. It usually includes an integrated development environment or a programming window, a debugger, a compiler, a visual editor, sample code and extensive documentation. |
| selector | This tells the web browser what particular HTML element(s) on a web page to apply a style rule. (See class selectors and id selectors.) |
| server | It is a system (software and suitable hardware) that manages access across a network to a centralized resource or network service. |
| skew() | This is a function provided as a value to the transform property and instructs the browser to slant an element a certain number of degrees to the right or to the left. |
| sliding door technique | This technique takes two or more images and displays them so that they appear to be one image of any size. |
| smartphone | A smartphone, as currently defined, has a multitasking operating system, a full desktop browser, wireless LAN (WLAN also known as Wi-Fi) and 3G/4G support, a music player and several of the following features: GPS or A-GPS, digital compass, video-capable camera, Bluetooth, touch support, 3D video acceleration, accelerometer, gyroscope, magnetometer. |
| sprite sheet | A sprite sheet is a single image which contains several different but identically sized images. |

| CSS Rules/ Terms | Definitions/Descriptions |
|---|---|
| static positioning | This means that the elements on a webpage will be displayed according to the normal top-down, left-to-right flow of HTML. Setting the top, right, bottom, left properties of an element will have no effect in static positioning. |
| tablet | A tablet has many of the same functionalities as a smartphone. It is a flat device that ranges in size from 7 to 11 inches and doesn't usually fit into a pocket. Tablets sometimes run a mobile operating system (iOS) or a touch-optimized version of a desktop operating system (Windows for tablets). |
| text-align | This property places a block of text to the left, right, or center of the page or container element. It can also left and right justify the text. Values for this property are: left, right, center, justify. |
| transform | This property rotates, scales (enlarges or reduces), skews, and even repositions an element while preserving its original margins so that the rest of the elements on the page are unaffected. Values to this property are the functions: rotate(), translate(), skew(), scale(). |
| transition | This is an animation of the changes made to the values of the properties of an HTML element over a specified period of time. For example, you can make a banner rotate a full 360 degrees over two seconds. CSS3 transitions are carried out by four transition properties: transition-property, transition-duration, transition-timing-function, and transition-delay. |
| transform (property) | Transition is also a property which bundles the four transition properties into one convenient style rule. In using the transition property, you list the other transition properties in a space separated list and in the order of property, duration, timing-function, and delay. For example, transition all 1s ease-in .5s. |

| CSS Rules/ Terms | Definitions/Descriptions |
|---|---|
| transition-delay | This property delays the start of an animation by a certain number of seconds or milliseconds. |
| transition-duration | This specifies (in seconds or milliseconds) how long it will take for the animation to complete. |
| transition-property | This specifies what properties of an HTML element to animate. |
| transition-timing-function | This transition property specifies the rate of the animation. (Do not confuse rate with duration.) Values for this property are: linear, ease (the default value), ease-in, ease-out, and ease-in-out. |
| translate() | This function is one of the values of the transform property and repositions an element from its current position in a webpage or container, by a set amount, to the left or right or up or down. |
| W3C | The World Wide Web Consortium, which sets specific standards for how CSS code (and other web languages) should be implemented by browsers. |
| white-space | This property describes how the space, tab, and new line characters (what we collectively call white-space) will be handled by the browser. Values for this property are: normal, pre, nowrap, pre-wrap and pre-line. |
| wrapping | Wrapping means that the text will automatically move (no need to start a new line by hitting the Enter key) to the next line when it reaches the right border of its containing element. |
| Z-index | This property determines the position of an element in a stack or layer of elements. It only applies to elements whose position property is set to either absolute, relative or fixed. |

# The Development Club

https://learntoprogram.tv/course/ultimate-monthly-bundle/?src=BOOKAD

This comprehensive membership includes:

• Access to EVERY course in LearnToProgram's growing library--including our exciting lineup of new courses planned for the coming year. This alone is over a $2,500 value.

• Access to our Live Courses. Take any of our online instructor-led courses which normally cost up to $300. These courses will help you advance your professional skills and learn important techniques in web, mobile, and game development.

• Free certification exams. As you complete your courses, earn LearnToProgram's certifications by passing optional exams. All certification fees are waived for club members.

• Weekly instructor hangouts where you can ask questions about course material, your personal learning goals, or just chat!

• Free Personal Learning Plans. You'll never wonder what you should take next to achieve your goals!

• The LearnToProgram guarantee!

THE LEARNTOPROGRAM GUARANTEE

**Our Guarantee:**
If you watch the course videos and complete the lab exercises, **you will learn to program**. Guaranteed. If you don't, we will personally pay your membership fees for the next 90 days.

The Development Club

Use Coupon Code: BOOK19
and get $20 off your first month!

More Information at
https://**LearnToProgram.tv**

www.ingramcontent.com/pod-product-compliance
Lightning Source LLC
Chambersburg PA
CBHW071545080326
40689CB00061B/1827